VISUAL COMMUNICATION
A WRITER'S GUIDE

Second Edition

Susan Hilligoss,
Clemson University

Tharon Howard,
Clemson University

New York Boston San Francisco
London Toronto Sydney Tokyo Singapore Madrid
Mexico City Munich Paris Cape Town Hong Kong Montreal

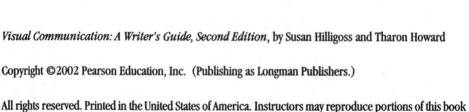

Visual Communication: A Writer's Guide, Second Edition, by Susan Hilligoss and Tharon Howard

ISBN: 0-321-09981-8

5 6 7 8 9 10 -   - 04

Contents

Acknowledgments

We are grateful to John Trimbur for his interest in Susan's visual communication seminar that led to the first edition of this book, and for the high example he has set in composition studies. For her enthusiasm and encouragement to make the first edition happen, Anne E. Smith has our sincere thanks. We also appreciate Lynn Huddon's efforts and support on this second edition. Donna Campion coordinated the process of putting together both editions with skill and tact. Leslie Taggart made a number of valuable suggestions. We also thank the College of Architecture, Arts, and Humanities and the Pearce Center for Professional Communication at Clemson University for use of the Multimedia Authoring Teaching and Research Facility.

We wish to recognize Christopher Lohr's efforts on the layout of the first edition and Wendy Howard's help proofreading the second edition. Bryce and Logan Howard gave their patience.

Permission to reproduce two flyers was given by the Department of Speech and Communication Studies, Clemson University. Thanks to the graduate students in Visual Communication for creating the genre graphics in Chapters 4, 5, and 8. Permission to reproduce their work is as follows: Amy Joy Bumgarner, makeover of speech lecture flyer; Keena Hamilton, typesetting of poem by William Wordsworth; Joseph D. Hooper, Kids newsletter; Ryan James Keith, original and makeover of presentation slides; Christopher Lohr, logo original and makeover, with comments, and portfolio pages; Rebecca J. Pope, makeover of speech club flyer and commentary; M. Esther Revis-Wagner, original and makeover of resumes; Deborah M. Staed, diagrams of whole page, body section, and navigation section of Web pages, with commentary, and original and makeover of Web pages; Myra A.Whittemore, grant proposal with budget, outcome graphic, and commentary; Michele Slater, storyboard for Web pages and tri-fold brochure; Sarah Weathers, Ceilbrite Web pages; Angela Davis, Aim High image poem; Parker Smith, tri-fold brochure and Livewire newsletter redesign. David Munger of Digital Text Construction, Davidson, NC, provided additional graphics. Our thanks to Barbara Heifferon for the example of the South Carolina Department of Transportation project. Susan's technical editing class, spring 1999, created the glossary and provided additional copyediting of the first edition.

Finally, we are indebted to many people for their contributions to visual rhetoric and document design, especially Stephen A. Bernhardt, Karen A. Schriver, Anne Wysocki, and Charles Kostelnick.

CHAPTER 1

Why Visual Communication for Writers?

In the past, college students wrote mainly essays and research papers seen by teachers and no one else. These papers were typed on typewriters, or "word-processed" and printed out on equipment that emulated typed text. They were formatted according to standards based on the manuscript preparation guidelines that college teachers used to submit their own writing to scholarly journals or presses.

Today, besides essays, college students write many other types of documents and consider readers outside the classroom. They prepare their work with sophisticated computers and printers that rival the output of commercial printing. They have many choices of fonts and the ability to incorporate drawings, charts, and graphs. They have access to a wealth of graphics via the Internet and inexpensive collections of clip art, as well as the means to create digital photographs and artwork. They make pages for the World Wide Web and effectively publish their work to a large audience. They collaborate with others, so that their documents present the *ethos* of a group, class, or organization to their readers. In short, the world of college writing has changed.

The visual design of the traditional essay or research paper, so long taken for granted, is only one of many "looks" that college writing may take. With so many choices, how should you, as a writer, make decisions about visual design? This guide is intended to provide strategies and numerous examples for you to consider.

What is visual communication?

In this guide, *visual communication* means all the ways that writers and readers interact through the look of pages and screens. *Visual design* means the structured process of planning for this interaction. There are other similar, overlapping terms. The widely used term *document design* covers much the same ground as visual communication, except that *document design* may also refer to matters of language, such as employing certain types of paragraph and sentence structure that have been shown to be easily understood by readers (Shriver 10; Felker et al. 1-2). *Communications design* and *information design* also refer broadly to visual communication.[1] In this guide, *texts*

1

and **documents** refer to both paper and on-screen writing. Likewise, **images** and **graphics** are used interchangeably for visuals that are distinct from verbal material.

Visual communication is part of the writer's task because the visual elements of a text affect how readers interact with the words. The interaction is rhetorical, and the importance of visual communication in documents is also supported by empirical research.

Visual communication is rhetorical

We can think of a document as a field of interacting rhetorical clusters.

Karen A. Shriver

Increasingly, documents are being regarded as more than words. Readers do not experience your written words in a vacuum. Typically you present your words on paper or on screen—that is, you **arrange** and **deliver** the text to readers. As soon as they encounter your text, readers immediately start to take in many kinds of visual information about it, from its apparent size to details of type, color, layout, and illustrations. As they continue to read or even just examine it, they use (and make judgments about) the visual design. Thus the design of a document is rhetorical, part of the interaction of writers and readers and contributing to effective communication. Consider visual design even during the early stages of your writing, **invention** and audience analysis. Good visual design clarifies a document's organization, called **arrangement** in classical rhetoric (Dragga and Gong 12). As for **style**, just as you choose your words to be "effective, appropriate, and striking," so may you choose images or visual design elements (Shriver 65). Design is also integral to effective presentation, known rhetorically as **delivery** (Dragga and Gong 14).

Visual design contributes to your **ethos** or credibility. Design that respects readers' knowledge supports a text's ethical appeal, while inappropriate format or jarring visual choices may make the document less credible.

Table 1.1 Visual communication and classical rhetoric	
Invention	Style
Arrangement	Delivery
Ethos	

In summary, when you plan the look of your document with your readers in mind, you engage in rhetorical thinking.

Visual design organizes readers' experiences of texts

Research in cognition, perception, and human factors psychology demonstrates that readers' understanding of texts is influenced by formatting and visual cues. Reading is a complex activity that relies on many layers of visual information.

How readers read. Studies of functional documents like manuals and forms have shown that readers do not read every word:

1. Readers are selective about what and how they read.
2. They read to accomplish their own purposes.
3. They actively interpret documents in light of their own knowledge and expectations.

Initially, readers decide what and how they will read. As Janice C. Redish, a researcher in document design and usability testing, declares, "Reading is a voluntary act; people don't have to do it" ("Understanding" 15). In the workplace, in public discourse, and at school, many documents compete for attention. Readers are compelled to be selective.

Once they decide to look at a document, readers do not necessarily read from start to finish. They scan, then read with their goals in mind—that is, they use the document as a tool to accomplish their own purposes. For example, in one study, readers of a manual read only two or three sentences at a time before they returned to the task at hand ("Understanding" 20).

Readers on the Web also scan for key words. A recent study showed that a large majority of test users scanned a new page rather than read word by word (Nielsen, "How Users Read on the Web"). This habit has implications for the look and organization of Web pages.

Finally, readers actively interpret as they read. Those interpretations are based on the words in front of them, but also on their past experiences and knowledge. As they read, people create mental models, or *schema*, of complex ideas. They also rely on their previous mental models. If readers' and writers' mental models of the document do not match—or writers do not make their own models of the document's features clear—readers may misunderstand portions of the document or even mistake its purpose.

Visual concepts contribute to readers' models. For example, in one case study, American readers used their training in document design and their knowledge of American companies' annual reports (their mental models based on past experience) as they examined Japanese annual reports translated into English. Yet their experience did not include design concepts familiar to Japanese readers and writers, who placed a high value on aesthetics and ambiguity (Maitra and Goswami 202). Thus, the American readers judged the Japanese reports in terms of their own mental models that required images to convey specific information and maintain cultural neutrality (202). They did not receive enough visual cues to interpret some images. They re-interpreted these to be "flashy" and nonfunctional (measured against their models), whereas to Japanese writers and readers, these images conveyed important values (200).

In another study, students aged 11 to 21 evaluated brochures on drug prevention for their effectiveness. They offered sophisticated evaluations of the choices of graphics, but found many of the visuals unpersuasive. Although the brochures were aimed at a teenage audience, the students considered the illustrations "'insulting'" or "'corny'" (Schriver 172). They pointed to the visuals that makes scanning and locating information convenient. Suggestions based on research findings include the following:

Table 1.2 Research-based visual strategies[2]

Queuing	Creating hierarchies of information
Filtering	Showing organization through design features such as headings, lists, typographic changes, layout
Color cueing	Using color to focus attention, simplify information, group elements, and create separate layers of information
Mixing modes	Giving information in pictures as well as words
Making schema explicit	Making clear the document model, such as a map of a Web site showing the relationships of pages
Creating multiple paths	Giving readers both verbal and visual choices through a document to support their different experiences and learning styles
User-centered design	Engaging readers in the process of designing documents through design reviews and usability testing

These are general strategies geared mainly to functional documents. In the following chapters, you will learn more about these and other strategies—and when and how to apply them for specific audiences and documents. Above all, researchers in document design wholeheartedly support the last strategy, ***user-centered design***. Regardless of suggestions, guidelines, and advice, writers should engage actual readers in the process of creating documents.

Using this guide

Good visual design complements good writing; it does not replace it. Together writing and design are part of finding the best available means to communicate with readers.

Tools. The explanations and examples in this guide assume that you can access and use a computer with "graphical" word processing software, such as Microsoft Word, WordPerfect for Windows, or Clarisworks. For paper documents either a laser or ink-jet printer is recommended; for Web documents, a graphical browser. Charts and graphs may require spreadsheet or presentation software; manipulation of images may require a paint or drawing program. Scanning requires a scanner and image editing software (such as Adobe Photoshop™). Examples are in black and white, although issues of using color—both print and onscreen—are explained. Even without specialized tools, you can create some types of effective visuals in paper documents by means of photocopying and pasting.

Skills and time management. Applying the techniques of good design takes time and effort. Give yourself ample time to learn and experiment before writing deadlines. Read the section on "drafts," then have others look at and comment on them.

Summary

- The changes in college writing affect the visual presentation of your documents.
- Visual communication is rhetorical, involving invention, arrangement, and delivery as well as contributing to ethos.
- Research with actual readers has implications for the visual design of documents.
- Don't expect visual design to substitute for good writing.
- As you experiment with design, do visual "drafts" and let others comment on them.

Notes

[1]Karen A. Shriver discusses definitions and competing terms for this field in "What Is Document Design?" *Dynamics in Document Design: Creating Texts for Readers* (New York: Wiley, 1997), pp. 1-11.

[2]Based on the following sources: Elizabeth Keyes, "Typography, Color, and Information Structure," *Technical Communication,* 40.4 (1993): 640-49; Janice C. Redish, "Understanding Readers," in Carol M. Barnum and Saul Carliner, *Techniques for Technical Communicators* (New York: Macmillan, 1993), 32, 36; Donald Norman, *The Design of Everyday Things* (New York: Doubleday, 1990) 187-217.

CHAPTER 2

First Impressions: Perception and Genres

What happens when we first view a document or image? Our eyes take in information, to be sure, but how do we make sense of what we see? Our perceptual abilities combined with our knowledge and past experience are involved. That is, we rely on the overall visual organization of materials plus our knowledge of text and graphical genres.

This chapter is about our first impressions when we take in visual information. It introduces ideas that are useful both in interpreting published visuals and in creating visual design. Here are two approaches for understanding our initial impressions of visuals: 1) the principles of perception, Gestalt psychology, and reading; and 2) rhetorical genres.

Visual perception

One approach to what we see comes from the psychology of sensation, perception, and memory. Vision takes in more sensory data than any other means of sensation. The eyes constantly move in small jumps in a process called *foveal vision*, which brings images into focus onto the area of clearest focus of the eye, the fovea. Then, in the process called perception, the brain interprets the data. Within hundredths of a second, the eyes can take in data that the brain processes in less than half a second (Coe 132-33).

However, we are not passive viewers. On the contrary, *visual perception* is an active, thinking process of planning for, as well as interpreting, sensory data from the eyes. That is, perception is a cognitive activity. In the terms of Rudolf Arnheim, an influential theorist of perceptual psychology and art, visual perception "is not a passive recording of stimulus material but an active concern of the mind" necessary for human survival (37).

The very fact that we direct our attention is an important part of visual perception. As we look around, we find *focal points*. A common example is walking into a room crowded with people. As we enter, we do not perceive everything in the room at once or equally. Instead, we tend to focus on a few items, such as a window, one small knot of people, or a person seated in a chair. In doing so, we ignore much of the other sensory information, a process called *filtering*. That filtering presumably "protects the mind from being swamped with" irrelevant information (Arnheim 25-26). As soon as we distinguish something in our field of vision, our past experience—including genre knowledge, which will be described later—comes into play, seizing on and interpreting the area of focus (Kostelnick and Roberts, 48-49). We use our vision to accomplish goals. We have an idea of what we will and want to see as we look around.

Readers take in a document's visual design and images immediately. ***Image memory***—that is, our memory of particular images as well as our own constructed "mental images" of pictures, events, and visual-related words—is also one of our most enduring types of memory (Coe 77). We apply lasting memories of images across the documents we encounter. Thus the design affects readers' first impressions of genre, interest, and importance. As they continue to look at the document, whether they are reading the entire text or scanning for important points, readers continue to gather information from the visual design, which can both structure their reading and supplement the text.

To summarize, "We see what we expect to see" describes the way that we plan and focus our attention visually. Many studies of eyewitness accounts of crimes confirm what Arnheim theorized: Our ability to focus comes with the ability to filter out visual information that does not seem relevant at the time, plus the ability to interpret what we do focus on only in terms of what is familiar to us. It helps to put this active, planning, filtering behavior into more memorable terms:

Table 2.1 Visual perception

We
forecast what we expect to see,
focus on a small area,
seek the **familiar,** and
tend to **filter** out other information.

That combination of forecasting, focus, familiarity, and filtering gives power to but also limits active visual perception. The process of planning, focusing, and filtering occurs over and over as we look around.

Being aware of these perceptual issues in visual communication can help you as you both interpret and create visuals for documents. One of the most important applications of perception to visual design arises from Gestalt psychology.

Gestalt principles

Gestalt is a German word that is translated as "form" or "wholeness" (Bevlin 15; Kostelnick and Roberts 53). The term describes an early 20th-century German movement in psychology. Gestalt psychologists studied many aspects of perception. In particular, they found that our perception of form depends not just on seeing individual parts but on the organization of the whole. In visual communication, the principles of Gestalt psychology are flexible, powerful tools for interpreting many kinds of visual information and for creating successful documents, pages, and screens.

Seeing the whole. When you look at this diagram, what do you see?

Figure 2.2 Visually ambiguous diagram

To many people, the dots suggest the corners of a square. However, they could just as easily be the endpoints of a large X. Gestalt psychologists created many experiments with visually ambiguous figures to study the ways that we organize visual information into wholes. Our tendency to structure ambiguous visual information fits with our forecasting, focusing perceptual behavior. Of the principles of Gestalt, two are especially helpful in interpreting and creating visuals in documents: 1) separating figure from ground, and 2) grouping by proximity and similarity.

Separating figure from ground. Our ability to see an image against a background is one of the most fundamental aspects of our visual perception. In Gestalt, this ability is called *figure-ground* separation. To go back to the example of walking into a crowded room, we use figure-ground separation to focus in on something or someone and then direct our steps toward that thing or person. In two-dimensional spaces like the page and the screen, we distinguish what is "on" the page or screen—blocks of text, headings, pictures—from the background, which continues "behind" the figure. In the following diagram, the smaller black rectangle appears to be "on" the larger white one.

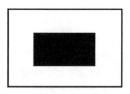

Figure 2.3 Figure-ground contrast

Ambiguous figure-ground contrast means that we cannot easily resolve what is placed in front and what is in back. In the classic visual puzzles of the Gestalt psychologists, this ambiguity is exploited by giving contradictory information about "unstable" figures to illustrate our tendency to resolve images into figure or ground. Stable figures tend to resist change based on the viewer's attention or the viewing conditions (Schriver 316).

However, in documents, ambiguous figure-ground separation is more often a result of too little information, not too much. Look at the boxed text below. What do your eyes focus on? The evenness of the text creates very little figure-ground contrast.

The term Gestalt describes an early 20th-century German movement in psychology. Gestalt psychologists studied many aspects of perception. In particular, they found that our perception of form depends not just on seeing individual parts but on the organization of the whole. In visual communication, the principles of Gestalt psychology are flexible, powerful tools for interpreting many kinds of visual information and for creating successful documents, pages, and screens. Our ability to see an image against a background is one of the most fundamental aspects of our visual perception. In Gestalt, this ability is called figure-ground separation. To go back to the example of walking into a crowded room, we use figure-ground separation to focus in on something or someone and then direct our steps toward that thing or person. In two-dimensional spaces like the page and the screen, we distinguish what is "on" the page or screen—blocks of text, headings, pictures—from the background, which continues "behind" the figure. In the following diagram, the smaller black rectangle appears to be "on" the larger white one. Ambiguous figure-ground contrast means that we have cannot easily resolve what is placed in front and what is in back.

Figure 2.4 Lack of figure-ground contrast

Even standard text conventions like word-spacing, upper- and lower-case letters, punctuation, and paragraphing assist with figure-ground separation. In ancient times, manuscripts were written in all capital letters. There was no spacing between the words and no punctuation, something like this:

**INANCIENTTIMESMANUSCRIPTSWEREWRITTENINALLCAPI
TALLETTERSTHEREWASNOSPACINGBETWEENTHEWORDSAN
DNOPUNCTUATIONSOMETHINGLIKETHIS**

Figure 2.5 The look of ancient text

Creating clear separations of figure and ground based on the rhetorical organization of the document is a good starting point for layout.

Grouping. The examples above show how we strive to relate disparate visual elements to create recognizable structures and wholes. One of the strongest ways to create relationships is by *grouping related items together*. We group in two main ways: by *proximity* and *similarity*.

Table 2.6 Grouping

What we observe	Gestalt principle
1. objects **close** to each other are related	*proximity (closeness)*
2. objects **similar** in shape, orientation, color, or texture are related[1]	*similarity*

Orientation refers to the object's direction—upright, horizontal, slanted, or rotated. *Texture* refers to any pattern on the object. Look at the following figure. Do you see four lines or two pairs of lines?

11

Figure 2.7 Proximity (closeness)

Look at the boxes below. Which items do you group?

 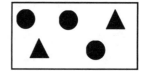

Figure 2.8 Grouping by closeness (1) and shape (2)

Figure 2.9 Grouping by orientation (3) and texture (4)

Proximity and *similarity* are the two most general and powerful grouping strategies.[2] We assume that even these abstract images are related just because they look alike or because they are located near each other. The basic *chunking* of text into short, visually distinct paragraphs relies on these grouping strategies. Lines of text are near enough to each other and have similar "footprints" of typography, size, length, and so on to be treated together.

These flexible strategies can be combined in many ways to create elaborate, subtle structures for displays and documents. For example, in a fact sheet about voter registration, you might decide to highlight important items with a check mark, like a mark on a paper ballot. You could make a list of such items:

12

✓ XXX XXXXX XXXXXX

✓ XXXX XX XXXXXX XX

✓ XXXX XXX XXXXX XXX

✓ XXXXXXX XX XXXXX

Figure 2.10 List of check marks

That visually groups the items by proximity and position on the page. Or you could scatter the check-marked items throughout the fact sheet. As long as the marks are bold and distinctive, readers will still tend to group them. Why? Because, as you can see, the eye tends to focus on these similar items regardless of their position.

XXXXXXXXXXXX XX XX✓XX

✓XXXXXXXX XXXXX XXXXX

XXXXXX XXXXXXXXXX XXX

XXXXX XXXXXXX ✓XXXXXX

XXXXXX XXXXXXXXXXX XXX

XXX XXXX ✓XXXXXX XXXX

Figure 2.11 Layer of scattered check marks

In other words, the check marks create a separate visual *layer* of information that can be viewed separately and scanned by itself while the remaining elements are *filtered* out (Keyes 640-41).

We also can combine grouping with standard Western layout conventions to create a visual hierarchy of information in a process called *queuing* (Keyes 640). Outlines use this process. We are accustomed to giving priority to the larger "high-level" headings and realizing that the smaller, "lower-level" type contains detailed information. In Figure 2.12, the bold headings all have the same size and weight ("color") of type, and they are all placed in the same relationship to the margin, paper edges, and other text. Despite the different words used in the headings, readers will treat them as visually similar. The italic headings will likewise be considered similar.

13

In addition, readers will assume that the bold headings are more immediately *important* than the italic headings because the bold takes up *more space* than the slender italic type. Westerners usually treat larger items as more significant than smaller items. If we wanted to heighten that difference, we could make the bold headings even larger or heavier. Readers can scan the bold layer, or at any time can revert to reading what is close by, in this case, the detailed text below the headings.

Gestalt

The term Gestalt describes an early 20th-century German movement in psychology. Gestalt psychologists studied many aspects of perception.

Figure-ground separation
Our ability to see an image against a background is one of the most fundamental aspects of our visual perception. In Gestalt, this ability is called figure-ground separation.

Stable figures: Stable figures tend to resist change based on the viewer's attention or the viewing conditions.

Unstable figures: Ambiguous figure-ground contrast means that we cannot easily resolve what is placed in front and what is in back.

Other principles
Our ability to relate items to each other forms the basis for other Gestalt principles.

Figure 2.12 Text layers and and hierarchy

Poorly grouped elements. How can you use grouping? One of the most common problems with documents is poor proximity. Logically related elements are visually separated from each other. For example, writers often use standard word-processing paragraph spacing—by pressing the ENTER key, for example—between blocks and headings, as in the sample from a fact sheet on the next page.

Why is there no bus service to the community center?

The original routes were scheduled before the community center was built.

Who is affected?

Everyone who uses the community center is impacted.

What can be done?

The center council has been meeting with city officials.

Figure 2.13 Evenly spaced text

To the reader, the even spacing means that the heading does *not* seem close to its text. Instead it "hangs" between the two paragraphs. A better solution is to have the heading sit closer to the text with which it belongs.

Why is there no bus service to the community center?
The original routes were scheduled before the community center was built.

Who is affected?
Everyone who uses the community center is impacted.

What can be done?
The center council has been meeting with city officials.

Figure 2.14 Headings close to following text

Even better, combine proximity and similarity by making the headings more like each other and less like the explanatory text.

Why is there no bus service to the community center?
The original routes were scheduled before the community center was built.

Who is affected?
Everyone who uses the community center is impacted.

What can be done?
The center council has been meeting with city officials.

Figure 2.15 Headings grouped by bold type

Using repetition and contrast. Similarity also suggests two other strategies. To make items similar we can *repeat* an element that they share. Likewise, to make different items stand out from each other and the background, we need to create clear *contrast*.

More on visual perception

Perception includes many other dimensions. A few that are helpful in interpreting and creating visuals are ordered perception, information zones, eye movement, and color.

Ordered perception. We readily distinguish the relative size of items and can quickly assign them an order or sequence—smallest to largest, or largest to smallest. Likewise, in a black and white illustration, we can point out the sequence of tones (or *values*) from black through shades of gray to white. We can also look at several patterns—such as dots or checkerboards—and order them by their *texture*, that is, the fineness or coarseness of their elements. We can apply size, value, and texture to aid readers in sequencing information (Bertin 67).

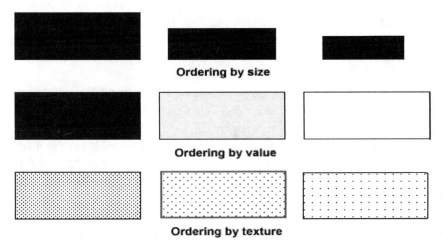

Ordering by size

Ordering by value

Ordering by texture

Figure 2.16 Visual ordering

Eye movement and brain processing. According to human factors experts, the eye moves most naturally from the upper left to the lower right of the visual field (Coe 259-60). This motion may somewhat counter the reading of text strictly horizontally, left to right. However, an eye-movement study by the Poynter Institute concluded that newspaper readers begin reading or "enter" a page wherever the strongest visual element is located. If the dominant visual was in the middle or lower half of the page, test readers began reading there (Baird et al. 6).

Color. Color is powerful and complex. It focuses attention like no other visual feature, and it outweighs other means of grouping (Bang 106). It moves viewers. Color can also distract and overwhelm. A color can mean one thing in one context and something completely different in another. A full discussion of color and perception is beyond the scope of this guide. However, here is a brief introduction. For guidelines on using color in documents, see Chapters 5 and 7.

Color has three perceptual dimensions, *hue*, *value*, and *saturation*:

- *Hue* is what we usually mean by color—blue, green, red, and so on.
- *Value* is the amount of black or white in a color. Printers add white to a hue to create tints, and black to create shades. Value is an important concept for designing documents.
- *Saturation* is the purity of a hue, often defined as the amount of color plus some amount of black, white, or gray. Bright red is highly saturated, while pink is not. Saturated colors retain their distinctiveness in bright light.

Although humans distinguish many colors (up to 7 million), we do not rank hues in any reliable order (Coe 147; Bertin 67). We do reliably place colors in order from lightest to darkest. That is, we rank them by *value.* (See the earlier discussion of ordered perception.) Value also helps us distinguish figure from background. We can pick out dark items on a light background or light items on a dark background, regardless of the actual hues.

Over the years research on color, especially as used in documents, has indicated that color helps readers find, organize, and make decisions about complex information. It can increase learning. Some colors also have physiological effects. In addition, the results of surveys show that computer users prefer color. Readers of advertising find color ads more memorable than black and white ads, while newspaper readers prefer bold color (Horton 223-5; Baird et al. 6).

Yet color also brings problems. Many problems result simply from overusing color and assuming that particular colors have set meanings for all viewers. Remember that different cultures assign very different social and emotional meanings to colors. For example, yellow indicates wildly different qualities in Western, Chinese, and Arabic cultures:

Table 2.17 Cultural differences with the color yellow

caution, cowardice	Western
honor, royalty	Chinese
happiness, prosperity	Arabic
	(adapted from Coe 150)

Overused, color also distracts attention for readers and can tire the eyes. There are many perceptual tricks that color plays on the eye, so that perception of any one color depends on nearby colors (Horton 227).

Color-vision deficiency affects 8 percent of males and 0.4 percent of females. People with color-vision deficiency may confuse red and green, confuse yellow and blue, or see only shades of gray (Coe 148). Documents that use color for important signals and organizational cuing should therefore accommodate readers for whom these signals may be unclear. See Chapters 5 and 7 for specific guidelines.

18

The psychology of seeing applied to documents

Western documents, arranged in pages or screens, divide material into text and pictures. There is evidence that the eye tends to focus on the illustrations before the text and notice pictures (representational illustrations) before more abstract illustrations (Dragga and Gong 171). Images are also easier to recall from memory than non-image data (Coe 77). Visual representations let us grasp spatial relationships and actions more quickly than verbal explanations do (Shneiderman 206-7). Further, people seem to have different ways that they learn best. Psychologists have divided these ways into *cognitive styles.* Learning primarily through visual means or imagination differs from the learning styles that emphasize analytical reasoning (Coe 57; Shneiderman 207). Our visual conventions are closely tied to language and experience. The presence of verbal cues influences how we interpret pictures.

Visual perception and reading

Reading itself certainly requires visual perception. Readers approach documents with one or more of five goals. They may want to:

- **skim** for the general meaning or gist of the whole document
- **scan** quickly for specific information
- **search** more thoroughly to comprehend specific information
- **read receptively** for thorough comprehension of the document
- **read critically** for evaluation of the document

(adapted from Coe 139-40)

Readers form goals as soon as they notice documents. Their genre expectations "kick in" as they notice the medium, format, and design. Visual information is critical to readers' meeting their goals as they proceed into the document. Let's examine the goals that readers have, using the example of a non-profit campus literacy organization.

Reading goals in action. Say that you and other students have created a brochure for the campus literacy organization that trains and places volunteer reading tutors. The brochure is designed to attract interest from students and sponsoring groups. Many readers will approach the brochure only to **skim** or **scan** it to understand basically what your organization does. They'll take in its images and some of its basic facts, then set it aside. The images may well establish the credibility of your organization, its ethos, in these readers' minds. Some will (at this time or later) **search** the brochure for specific information, such as a phone number. No one expects a brochure to cover a topic in depth, so it makes a quick visual and rhetorical impression. At the same time, it makes a few well-chosen facts easily accessible. Visual design is important to both purposes.

Reading goals and visual design. As readers approach your document, visual design and other elements of the document, especially the arrangement of text, intertwine. Readers of the literacy brochure use visual design and information to accomplish set, often rather limited, goals. Charles Kostelnick and David D. Roberts note that *"We use vision to complete the task at hand—and little more"* (50; authors' italics). They rely on previous knowledge to interpret your document visually, and where that knowledge is not yet generalized (as in Web sites), they rely on pattern and consistency to interpret what they see. From visual elements they also infer qualities of the organization and the writer—ethos—even to the point of making judgments. Our prior knowledge of visuals leads us to the discussion of genres.

Genres and visuals

As we look, we focus on the familiar and filter the rest. What then is familiar? In part it is our accumulated memories and experience, including our mental models (schemata). These mental models are highly organized into networks and categories of information, so that we can recognize many visual forms, from photographs to types of documents, almost instantaneously. As readers, publication designers, and writers, we constantly act on that recognition. The idea of *genre knowledge* is helpful in understanding how these larger visual and document forms operate.

Genre knowledge. *Genres*, which are kinds of discourse or documents like poems, persuasive essays, or news articles, have different goals and proceed differently. Rhetorically, genres are not just forms of texts but also "socially active devices" (Jolliffe 279; Miller 151). That is, knowledge of genre helps readers determine what the writer wants from them as they read and helps them to read successfully and purposefully (Jolliffe 279-80). For example, readers approach a poem with certain expectations. They bring very different expectations to reading an essay of political argument, a resume, a magazine profile, a brochure, or a consumer guide. As defined in this guide, our *genre knowledge* consists of networks of mental models or schemata that we have created from repeated experiences.

Readers make genre decisions early and use a variety of types of information to do so. Some information is language-based. The conventional phrase "Once upon a time" signals a fairy tale—or a variant of that genre—to many people raised to speak and read English. In fact, this phrase is a verbal *convention*, one of "the customary forms and configurations that members of an audience expect" to appear in a given example of a genre (Kostelnick and Roberts 33).

Much genre information is non-verbal. Many genres *look* different from each other: a novel, a yearbook, a magazine, a newspaper. Newsletters have many of the same visual features as newspapers but have a recognizable format of their own. Sonnets have a characteristic "boxy" look on the page. In fact, simply looking at a text or a portion of a document may help us to classify it, so that we know what to expect even before reading. Compare, for example, Figures 8.1 and 8.9.

As we interpret what we are looking at, we also position ourselves and the document in relation to the writers, artists, or designers. We may decide that we are looking at a very old poem or painting, or one that was created in a different culture from ours. Within the image we may find other ways to relate to the producers. For example, we may find represented figures sympathetic. This interpersonal response is a part even of abstract images and diagrams (Kress and Leeuwen 41). Or, like the students reading anti-drug use brochures in Chapter 1, we may feel disconnected from the document's authors.

Genre knowledge is held in common by groups of readers and writers called *discourse communities*. These communities may be large or small, and we all belong to a number of shifting, overlapping discourse communities.

How are genres and reading goals related? Genre and visual perception interact complexly during reading. Through the literacy brochure's folded format and design, readers quickly take in the fact that is it *is* a brochure—and expect it to contain certain types of information. Almost as soon as they see it, readers use the brochure's visual features to make moment-by-moment decisions—to keep reading, for example—and to make judgments about the credibility of the group and the usefulness of the information. Try this out by examining the brochure in Figure 8.17 and keeping track of what visual features attract your attention.

What are visual conventions or practices? As with verbal knowledge, our visual knowledge of genres is made up of many clustered bits of knowledge and expectations—visual *conventions* or *practices* or simply features. These clusters operate at all levels of detail. Large-scale features include the size and weight of paper or printed stock that the publication uses. A newspaper uses newsprint, easily identifiable by its texture and size (and feel). At the medium level of page layout, there is the convention that newsletters and newspapers usually have multiple columns while reports and academic essays have exactly a one-page-wide "column." On a smaller scale, the acceptable format for business letters specifies the spatial organization of the text. Each element has a place: date, inside address, salutation, body, closing, signature block, and the like. We only need to glance at a piece of paper to make an initial decision about what it is and how it relates to our purposes. That is the power of visual conventions.

Based on other cues, we are able to understand and correctly apply two or more different conventional interpretations of the same visual element. For example, in a research paper, superscript numbers indicate footnotes or endnotes. Yet in mathematical text, superscripts indicate exponents (the "power" to which a variable is raised).

One common type of ancient map is the strip map.[2]

$$x^2 + y^2 = z^2$$

Figure 2.18 Same symbol, different meanings

The same visual element has two conventional meanings. We use the context to determine which interpretation to apply. If the writers have not used the superscript convention in the same way that we understand it, we will be confused and frustrated.

Whose practice is it? A particular visual convention may be standard within a certain group and part of its local culture. For example, many companies and agencies distinguish between types of stationery used for different types of documents. In fact, writers at one organization routinely called one set of documents that they wrote "pink memos" and another set "white memos" because the two verbal genres were also distinctive visually (Odell, Goswami, Herrington, and Quick 21). Other visual conventions are much more widespread.

In page and screen layout, for example, readers of Western languages recognize these conventions:

- text will read from top left to bottom right
- larger items are more significant than smaller items
- items higher on the page have more priority than those lower down
- signals of continuation ("more to come") appear at bottom center or bottom right

(Kristof and Satran 90)

Another example is the slashed circle as an international symbol for "prohibited."

**Figure 2.19 This widespread visual convention means
an activity is prohibited.**

It is a mistake, however, to assume that "widespread" means "universal." Visual symbols, in particular, require care in their use. Many apparently "universal" symbols are not understood at all, or are understood in ways completely unintended by the writer or designer. Nor should particular images, symbols, or visual techniques be automatically labeled "natural" or "lifelike." As the art historian E. Gombrich has shown, much of the visual "language" of drawing and painting is not based on life, but on other drawings and paintings (65, 75-77). Over time we realize that these so-called lifelike renderings employ techniques that are more local than universal.

What previous visual knowledge do designers and viewers share? If you have ever played the game PICTIONARY®, you know that it does not take much artistic skill.[3] Success depends on how fast you can tap into your team's previous visual knowledge. The same applies to all pictures, images, and illustrations. Look at the following picture:

Figure 2.20 These visual conventions indicate gender and relationship.

The visual conventions to indicate gender are fairly clear to Western readers. The sizes of the shapes plus the joined arms indicate a relationship of *mother and **daughter***.

Let's try another. Say that the word to illustrate is ***spinach***. You try this:

Figure 2.21 Spinach?

Is it clear that this image is supposed to be spinach? Probably not, so you try:

Figure 2.22 Spinach?

Think your team will get it? Finally you sketch:

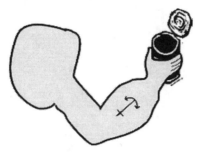

Figure 2.23 A visual association for spinach

24

In American popular culture, spinach is associated with the cartoon character Popeye, and Popeye has a characteristic look, including huge forearms.[4] Could you do the same with another green, leafy vegetable such as **kale** or **collards**? Probably not. Visual conventions can be highly specific, with unique associations in viewers' experiences.

How flexible is this practice? Is the visual feature required, in effect a rule? If so, that convention is strict (Kostelnick and Roberts 34). Business letters have a strict format, as do many types of academic papers and resumes. On the other hand, the formats of newsletters and brochures are relatively flexible. Within certain expectations, the creators of newsletters and brochures have considerable freedom to adapt the look. There is a limit to the freedom, however. Even within flexible genres and conventions, readers still need enough quick visual information to identify the document's genre and accomplish their reading goals.

However, even rigid conventions can change. Those who use a convention often face new needs and so they adapt existing genre knowledge.

Visual practices change. Like business letters, workplace memoranda have fairly rigid visual conventions. Letters and memos differ a great deal in where they place routing and subject information. In memos, all routing or classifying information goes in the top heading. In particular, in business letters you as sender put your name at the bottom (and nowhere else), whereas in memos you put your name at the top on the FROM: line (and nowhere else.)

Box Y5555
Clemson University
Clemson, SC 29634

January 18, 1999

Mr. Henry Collins
Literacy Project
1151 Main St.
Pendleton, SC 29670

Dear Mr. Collins:

Thanks for agreeing to speak with our peer tutor group. The meeting is 7 pm in the conference room on and we meet brn 6:45? That will the setup of the room and ask me questions. In time, please call if you need any information. My phone number is 864.555.5555.

We all look forward to your visit.

Sincerely,

Leslie Jene

Leslie M. Jene

```
TO: Peer tutors
FROM: Leslie M. Jene, student coordinator
SUBJECT: Monthly meeting
DATE: January 21, 1999

Our next meeting is Monday, February 1, at 7 pm in the library confer-
ence room. The speaker will be Henry Collins, head of the Literacy
Project for Anderson County. Mr. Collins will talk about the county's
program that currently has over 100 high school and middle school
students involved in tutoring younger children.

Please send additional agenda items to me at Box Y5555 or
864.555.5555.
```

Figure 2.24 Memo and letter formats

Electronic mail formats are based on memos, with the routing information (which also serves as the electronic envelope) at the top, separate from the body. Yet e-mail users found that some mail systems did not identify them except by their short "userIDs," and recipients were sometimes confused about who sent the message. E-mail users began attaching "signature files" or "sig files" to the bottom of the body of their messages. That is, they identified themselves as senders both at the top and bottom of the e-mail.

As e-mail has become widespread, the convention of putting the sender's name at both top and bottom of a message is now increasingly seen in paper memoranda. The change is not yet widely accepted—it is not a new convention. The discourse communities that see value in the old practices for memoranda insist on having all routing information at the top. Many regard the bottom signature on memos as simply wrong. But over time, the conventions for all of these genres may adapt because of the introduction of e-mail. As Carolyn Miller has noted, genres evolve and decay (153).

```
DATE:   Thurs 21 Jan 99 14:48:03
TO: zygg@clemson.edu
FROM: ljene@clemson.edu
SUBJECT: meeting?

z.,

What're you doing tonight? I tutor until 8, but
after that I'm free. We could start brainstorm-
ing some ideas for the project. How's the new
room? I'll check e-mail till 4. After that call
me. ;)

L.

----------------------------------------------------
"The flow of the river is ceaseless and its
water is never the same." -- Kamo no Chomei
----------------------------------------------------
Leslie M. Jene                     864.555.5555
Box Y5555, Clemson University Clemson, SC 29634
```

TO: Peer tutors
FROM: Leslie M. Jene, student coordinator
SUBJECT: Monthly meeting
DATE: January 21, 1999

Our next meeting is Monday, February 1, at 7 pm in the library conference room. The speaker will be Henry Collins, head of the Literacy
Project for Anderson County. Mr. Collins will talk about the county's
program that currently has over 100 high school and middle school
students involved in tutoring younger children.

Please send additional agenda items to me at Box Y5555 or
864.555.5555.

Sincerely,

Lesley

Figure 2.25 E-mail with sig file; memo with signature

How can you learn more about visual practices? As the e-mail example shows, when we
are faced with a new visual (or other) element, one response is to say it is wrong. It goes against
the rules, we say. Or it is not "proper" or "appropriate." That is how genre knowledge works.
But to increase your visual awareness, consider who holds this rule or convention in common
and how flexible or rigid they consider it to be. In other words, consider the discourse community or, more likely, communities who understand this visual convention. If you can, ask someone who appears to belong to the community to state her understanding and preferences. Ask
anyone who has to read and write in the workplace what is proper memo and e-mail format.
Ask how far these formats can be bent before the changes affect the reader's judgment of the

27

writer. Then go to other people and ask the same questions. Note where their statements overlap and where they diverge, and consider why that might be the case, based on the discourse communities to which you think they belong.

Visual practices are complex and fluid. Knowledge of genres and specific visual conventions helps us negotiate the complex world of documents that we encounter. A large part of this book is devoted to increasing your knowledge of specific visual practices. However, there is no attempt to develop a system of classification of visuals. Because of the complexity of visual information as well as the open nature of genres, that would be a difficult and probably pointless task (Miller 151-53). Genre knowledge is fluid, at times contradictory, and subject to change. As you develop your awareness, consider that our genre knowledge sometimes limits as well as helps us. Part of learning is learning where and how to apply knowledge, plus learning the extent and influence of discourse communities that sanction this knowledge.

Conclusion: visual perception, practices, and genres. For many reasons, some experts are now recommending that visual information make up a fairly large proportion of pages and especially screens. Genres that require much skimming and searching, such as instructions, manuals, and online documentation, have up to half or more of their information in visual form, which includes layout features and the blank or "white" space used to frame blocks of information (Coe 221). Other genres are also becoming more visual, to motivate, convey ethos, and aid readers in understanding.

Summary

- Visual perception is an active process of planning and fulfilling expectations about what we are viewing. Visual perception is extraordinarily fast and involves the brain almost from the start.
- As we look, we focus on the familiar and tend to filter out the rest.
- The Gestalt principles of 1) figure-ground separation and 2) grouping by proximity and similarity help explain our perception of complex pages and screens.
- Knowledge of visual practices involves knowing who employs them and how flexible the practices are.
- Visual information is becoming more prevalent in many genres.

Exercises

1. Consider the "junk mail" that you receive. How do you determine it is junk? That is, what cues do you use to classify it as the genre of junk mail (or direct marketing solicitation, to use the industry term)? Which cues are visual, like the large-size envelopes and colorful inserts? Which are language-based, like the method of addressing you? Which are tactile? What features does junk mail share with other mail, such as bills or business envelopes that contain new credit cards? Given the subtleties that some direct marketers use, how do you make the determination without wasting much time? Consider your reading goals and moment-by-moment decision-making as you examine a piece of mail. What visual information contributes to your decisions to stop or to continue reading?

2. With a partner or small group, try "drawing" the words below. Discuss the differences between your drawings and what visual features play a part in each. Try sketching other words and have your partner or group members guess the words from the sketches. What features matter most?

sky	**cape**	**map**
tree	**homeless**	**modern art**
oak	**yield**	**philosophy**

3. The World Wide Web is relatively new, yet immensely popular. Do you think that the discourse communities of Web users have created distinctive visual genres? That is, are there clearly different kinds of sites based on visual information? Try the following. Identify several types of Web sites. Then compare them visually: number and types of images, moving or static imagery, use of color, number, and types of visually distinct areas on the screen, type styles, format of text. How would you evaluate these differences?

Notes

[1]These are four of Jacques Bertin's six "retinal variables." He states that these four, shape, texture, orientation, and color, have "associativity" (Bertin 65).

[2]Mullet and Sano 95. Although they are the most important for our purposes, figure-ground separation, proximity, and similarity are only three of the Gestalt principles. The others include

closure, continuation, symmetry, and *common fate*. Good discussions of Gestalt theory for designers and writers appear in Mullet and Sano (91-93), Schriver (303-26), Coe (18-23), and Kostelnick and Roberts (53-70). Robin Williams has worked out a design method based in part on Gestalt principles in *The Non-Designer's Design Book*.

[3]PICTIONARY® is a commercial game similar to the parlor game "Charades," in which teams guess words from quick sketches rather than gestures. PICTIONARY® is a registered trademark of Pictionary Incorporated under license to Hasbro, Inc.

[4]Popeye the Sailor is a copyrighted character of King Features Syndicate.

CHAPTER 3

Second Impressions: Interpreting Images and Information Graphics

Typically as we examine documents, we resolve what we see into words and "pictures."[1] As Chapter 2 has shown, we tend first to focus on the pictures—visual elements like photographs, drawings, maps, or graphs. The array of pictures that we encounter in print and on computer screens is vast and complex. The ability to analyze and interpret visuals in our culture is sometimes called *visual literacy*. Visual literacy includes not just understanding the basics of visual information and persuasion, but also the potential for distortion.

This chapter concerns the interpretation of pictures, meaning anything on the page or screen that is set off to be looked at. The pictures may also contain words and call on us to read, but they have additional dimensions. Pictures can be divided into:

1. Images—including photographs, lifelike or stylized drawings, cartoons, and combinations of these with each other and with text, as in advertisements

2. Information graphics—including maps, diagrams, tables, charts, and graphs.

In this chapter, you will find strategies for making sense of common types of images and information graphics. For more about using them in your own documents, see Chapter 7.

Making sense of images

Images call on our perceptual and genre knowledge, including many specific visual conventions, plus our emotional responses. This discussion concerns still images, but much of it also applies to moving images on television, film, and the Web. Common types of still images include news and documentary photographs, conceptual photographs, drawings, clip art, cartoons, and advertisements in print and on the Web.

News and documentary photographs

When we say an image looks real, we often use our knowledge of photographs as a yardstick. The 35-millimeter color photograph has been called the standard of realistic representation in our time (Kress and van Leeuwen 163). That reputation has been honed by a century of newspaper and documentary photography, which "records events or faithfully shows the reality of people or places" (Finberg and Itule 227). *News and documentary photos* are spontaneous or near-spontaneous recordings of human events and conditions, ranging from news events to sports to daily life. Professional news and documentary photos are serious visual compositions with the potential for great emotional and social impact. To maintain their credibility, these photographs can only be edited or manipulated in certain ways, such as being *cropped*, that is, having extraneous details cut off. Like all visuals, news and documentary photographs are selective and subject to manipulation. However, photojournalists and news photo editors have an ethical responsibility to let the photographic image tell the viewer an informative and full story—as well as an interesting one (Finberg and Itule 197, 226).

Conceptual photographs

Photo illustrations or *conceptual photographs* are posed or manipulated to make a point. Conceptual photography also includes many pictures taken to illustrate news, feature stories, art photography, and all advertising photography. The photograph is often staged, manipulated or edited to make the point more clearly. Stunt photos—for example, having your picture taken at a carnival behind a prop showing a monster's body—are obviously conceptual. So are the results of "morphing" software that transform photos digitally. So are news photos that are manipulated and edited beyond basic journalistic practice. The 27 June 1994 cover of *Time* magazine showing O. J. Simpson as darker-skinned and more heavily bearded—and possibly more menacing—than in the original photo is another example. Professional photographers who exhibit their work also employ concepts, often to raise questions about our acceptance of photographic reality. Conceptual photos have many worthwhile uses, if their purposes are understood.

You probably have also seen *stock photographs*, standardized conceptual images from commercial data bases. Stock photos are sold as backgrounds for annual reports, ads, brochures, and many other documents. In addition to lending a professional polish to a document, these images may create moods and portray themes.[2] Stock photographs are also available in common word processing and desktop publishing programs, as well as on the Web. Although they are often more sophisticated than clip art, stock pictures have many of the same drawbacks.

Conceptual pictures represent reality, in a way—but only in a way. Their impact comes from the blending of apparent photographic reality with many subtle or arresting visual effects.

Drawings, cartoons, clip art

Drawings have an enormous range—from detailed pen and ink illustrations to colorful *icons* (small, stylized images often used for links and "buttons" in software). In this electronic age, many drawings are not actually drawn by hand, but rather created with computer illustration programs by graphic artists. With photographs as the standard of reality, we often do not expect drawings to be particularly lifelike or realistic. (An exception is scientific and technical illustrations, which are expected to be as accurate as possible.)

In fact, the popular genres of drawings—cartoons and comic strips—exaggerate for the sake of humor. Computers and the Web have made huge collections of colorful drawings available electronically. These collections are called *clip art*, from the print books that originally were the source of these images. Much clip art is available for fair use (see Chapter 7). Because it is so widespread, clip art is influential. For the same reason, it can be trite and overused. Worse, clip art can perpetuate gender, racial, and cultural stereotypes.

Remember that norms for images change over time. The changes may be particularly apparent in drawings. For example, for years the U. S. Army has published a monthly magazine devoted to vehicle maintenance updates. Its comic-book appearance, many illustrations, and sexy female characters interest soldier-mechanics who are mostly male and who are not necessarily proficient or well-motivated readers. But the sexual appeal has changed over 20 years. An issue from 1970 features a continuing female character in a mini-skirt and halter top. In a 1990 issue, the female characters, now of different ethnic backgrounds, dress in fatigues. In addition, the drawings no longer look like part of the counter-culture of the 1960's. The more obvious visual sexism and outdated art have been "toned down" to suit a volunteer professional Army that has more women and is more aware of gender and racial bias (Bernhardt 217).

Print and Web advertisements

Advertising makes use of all kinds of images, such as conceptual photographs, drawings, and reproductions of paintings and sculpture, to name just a few. Each ad also arranges visual elements in a space and sequence designed to persuade the potential buyer. Advertising is one of the chief sources of visual images and design for many people; it literally defines much of what we know about visual communication. The field of graphic design owes its growth to advertising and corporate communications (see Chapter 9).

The art historian and cultural critic John Berger has said that advertising creates an alternate reality, inviting us to envy advertising's dream world and seek its glamour, which he defines as the happiness of being envied by others (132, 142). He also notes how sophisticated our genre knowledge is. In a magazine, we are generally able to distinguish ads from news articles and features, despite the fact that they are placed together and employ many of the same visual features, such as photographs (151-52). Yet many advertisers seek to blur the line between the document's editorial content and the ads.

The Web is also a commercial environment. Because it is relatively new, the conventions for the placement and look of ads are not completely settled. Newcomers to the Web may be tempted by links that appear to be part of a page's contents, only to find that the links take them to a commercial product or service.

Analyzing images

Try asking the following questions when you analyze an image, whether it is a news or documentary photograph, a conceptual photo, an ad, a cartoon, a comic strip, a line drawing, or a piece of clip art. Not all the questions will apply, of course, but many will be relevant. Extend your analysis of those answers that seem most important.[3]

Rhetorical purpose—images

- Where does this image appear?
- What is the image's purpose? Does it document a situation, event, or condition? Is it conceptual? If so, what is its point? Does it specifically support an appeal to buy something?
- Is the image realistic, like a photograph? Or more stylized, like a cartoon or caricature?
- If the image is realistic, do you detect any types of distortion? Describe any features that may be distorted.
- How polished or "professional" is the image?
- What tone does the image project?
- How seriously do you take it? Explain why.

- Who do you think are the intended viewers of this image? What features suggest that audience?
- Who do you think produced this image? Is the creator or photographer stated?
- What would you say your relationship is to the producer or producers? Do you think they understand you as a viewer?

Overall design

- What draws your eye first?
- What does the dominant part of the image portray?
- What is in the center of the image?
- What is shown in front and larger? What is behind and smaller?
- What is shown in the upper half? The lower half?
- Are portions more blurred? Are there very distinct parts in sharp focus?

   We respond to what we think is the dominant area, in sharp focus. The center of the visual field—page or screen—is one common area of emphasis. We may also tend to place more emphasis on what is larger (in front) and in the upper half. Would you say this is true in this image? How so?

- On a sheet of paper, draw or trace the major areas of the image and label them.
- Is there empty space? What does the empty space "frame"?
- Are some areas or shapes very large? Are others very small?

   We respond to extremes of scale. Not only do huge areas seem very close while tiny ones seem far away, but together the two extremes may suggest tension or conflict. For example, a small outline of a child placed on a large white background may suggest to us that the child is alone and vulnerable, at odds with the vast background, or just less significant than the background.

- Describe the major shapes and lines created. Consider what effect the shapes and lines create.

   According to some who study psychology and art, "Smooth, flat, horizontal shapes give us a sense of stability and calm" (Bang 56). Vertical lines, defying gravity, suggest energy and activity, while diagonal lines create tension and interest, moving off the page or screen in a clear direction. Circles are the ultimate in symmetry and may be considered both dynamic and static, completely in balance.

35

- Describe the overall arrangement of parts. Are they ordered symmetrically or otherwise balanced against each other?
- Would you say that the parts form an array of smaller images, like a yearbook page? In what order do you look at these? Or are they a sequence to be read as a story? Does the arrangement convey anything about the purpose of the image?

People

- Who is portrayed? Describe your inferences from each feature of the person(s)—age, details of dress, gender, ethnicity, class, posture and stance, portions of the body shown, tilt of head, facial expression, gesture of hands.
- What is the person looking at? Follow her or his "gaze" or "eyeline." Does he or she look toward something else in the image? Or out of the picture toward the viewer? What do you make of the direction of the gaze?
- If there are two or more people, what features suggest their relationships to each other?
- If there are two or more people, does one seem dominant? How is that expressed?
- As with shapes in general, people who are larger (take up more area of the image) or are placed "above" other people may seem more dominant.
- From what angle are the people shown? Do you seem to look down on them, as if they were below you as viewer? Look up to them? Look right at them?

   In film studies, the angle of viewing suggests the relationship between the viewer and the people portrayed. If we as viewers "look down" on people, they may seem powerless or helpless. On the other hand, looking up to them makes them seem powerful, even domineering (Giannetti and Langdon 45). At eye level, neither above nor below us, they appear more "at our level" of power and freedom.

- Are the people shown close up? Far away?

   In an image, people's apparent distance from the viewer suggests emotional distance. For example, a close-up of someone's face may make us feel more emotionally involved with the person—and the image as a whole. Extreme close ups may also seem cramped or claustrophobic.

- What do you consider to be your relationship as viewer to the person or people shown? Do you empathize with them or not? Explain why.

- If there is no one represented, imagine what sort of person would be at home in this image. Explain why.

Setting

- If the image has a distinctive background, describe it. How does it relate to the dominant focus of the image—especially people, if any?
- What time and place does the image suggest? What is the effect of that setting?
- Is anything "out of place" in the image? Is a horse shown inside a house, for example? What do you make of the incongruity?

Symbols and signs

- Are there items or features in the image that "mean more than themselves"? Consider the connotations and associations of particular objects or features in the image. Then relate them to the rest of the image.

    Objects like a flag, a cross, and a six-pointed star are obvious symbols. However, language and visuals are filled with signs, things that stand for someone or something else. We associate emotion-laden concepts with particular sensory features, and they become signs, or stand-ins for those concepts and emotions. For example, cosmetics ads draw on cultural anxieties about aging and attractiveness. In the context of moisturizing products, dryness can become "a metaphor for loss of sexual attractiveness," with dry skin standing in for the whole woman past her youth and sexual prime (Berger 188).

Color

- Describe the colors, or absence of color, in the image.
- Where is color is applied?
- Is the color realistic in your view? If not, describe why you think it is not.
- How does color, or its absence, make you feel about the image?
- What previous associations do you have with the colors used? How do those affect your understanding of the image?

Text

♦ If the image includes text—such as headlines, labels, captions, or paragraphs of explanation—relate the text to the image.

♦ In what ways does the text help you make sense of the image? Does it answer questions about the image, or only raise more questions?

♦ What is the personality and tone of the typography—the fonts that the text uses? (See Chapter 6 for more on fonts.)

Story

♦ What is the story being told in the image? Consider the people and objects in the image and their relationships to each other, the viewer, and the setting, and the text.

♦ Who can relate to this story? Who may not find it believable or interesting?

♦ Who or what is excluded from this image? Why do you think that?

♦ What attitudes—social, political, economic, cultural—are suggested in this image? Who benefits from the attitudes shown? Who doesn't?

Look at illustration 3.1. Using some of the questions on rhetorical purpose, overall design, people, and story, what can you say about this image?

Figure 3.1 An image for analysis

In sum, examine an image rhetorically and critically. Locate yourself in relationship to the images. Consider how the parts of the image interact, but also consider the world outside the image.

Making sense of information graphics

Every day as readers we constantly encounter factual information displayed in tables, charts, graphs, and maps. In newspaper and magazine articles, these *information graphics* summarize key points and often make dry, abstract information more compelling. In the social and physical sciences, a research paper's most convincing evidence for its argument may be in its *data displays*.[4] These visual arrays open a dynamic space for discovering relationships among abstract ideas and thus creating knowledge (Bolter 77). Information graphics—tables, charts, graphs, and maps—use our powerful abilities of visual discrimination to compare, notice trends, and understand complex relationships among parts.

We also expect these graphics, like news photographs, to give accurate, undistorted representations of the world. However, all information displays are selective. That is part of their ability to show clearly certain aspects of the data. Because they are selective, they are also subject to distortion and manipulation. They can obscure data, misrepresent relationships among the data, and even suggest biased conclusions. The following sections describe common types of information graphics, then suggest strategies for making sense of them and spotting possible distortions.

Tables

Tables arrange information into columns and rows. (Strictly speaking, most tables are not graphics at all, but they display information more visually than text does.) Tables use a grid structure to help the eye locate and compare bits of information.

Making sense of tables. Here is a table showing numbers of students living in three dorms over the course of three semesters:

Table 3.2 How many students in dorms?

	Fall	Spring	Summer	Total, 98-99
East Dorm	400	380	120	900
West Dorm	250	270	115	635
South Dorm	345	415	45	804
Term totals	995	1065	280	2339

The title gives the purpose of the table while the orderly presentation lets us compare across, by dorm, or down, by term. The top row gives important information in the **column headings**, while the far left column (called the **stub**) labels the rows. We can see that East Dorm has the greatest number of students in total. We can see that spring term has the highest number of dorm residents while summer has the least. South Dorm had the highest number of students for any term—spring—a fact that is somewhat buried (see Figure 3.3 for comparison).

Distortion. Complex tables may obscure data, and simple ones may omit important data. However, tables are not subject to the visual distortions that plague graphical displays. Poor tables may not be well labeled or set up for easy comparison.

Charts and graphs

Charts and graphs plot numbers into visual form.[5] Most common charts use two dimensions, the horizontal (the **x-axis**) and the vertical (the **y-axis**). Different charts show data differently. Here are a few standard types:

Bar charts compare values across categories. They are good at showing how proportions are related to each other—but not total numbers. In the example, the categories are the three dorms gathered by terms. The length of the shaded bars representing the different dorms' students can easily be compared. South Dorm's high spring total and low summer total are more evident here.

Dorm occupancy by term

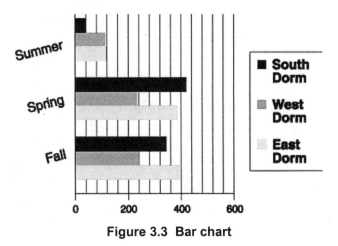

Figure 3.3 Bar chart

When the bars are vertical, it becomes a *column chart*, which allows convenient comparison over time.

Dorm occupancy by term

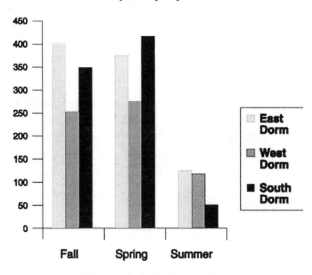

Figure 3.4 Column chart

41

Line graphs show trends, usually over time. Would you say that the progression from fall to spring to summer term is continuous? The line graph, which connects the three terms, assumes that there is a smooth progression. This version may wrongly emphasize a downward trend in occupancy. Summer dorm residency is probably a different category—always low.

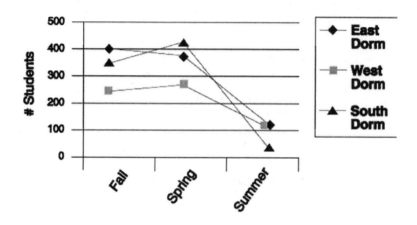

Figure 3.5 Line graph

Some charts allow us to see the total numbers more easily. *Pie charts* are well-known for showing how a single whole is divided into parts. However, we cannot easily tell precise amounts from these shapes. Pie charts are best for showing a few segments that differ significantly from each other. They must be labelled with percentages if we are to comprehend precise differences.

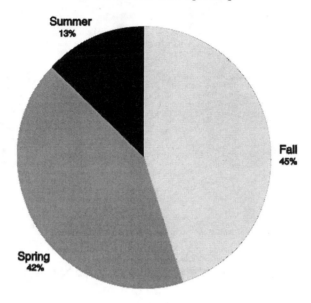

Figure 3.6 Pie chart

Stacked column charts and *stacked area charts* let us see both the individual components—the dorms in this case—and their contribution to the total number per term. They allow us to look across the stacks to follow one dorm, or look at the height of the stack at any point.

Total dorm occupancy by term

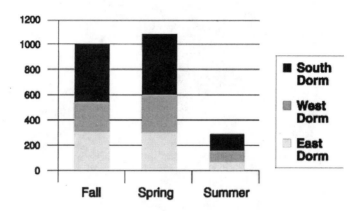

Figure 3.7 Stacked column chart

Overall change in occupancy, all dorms

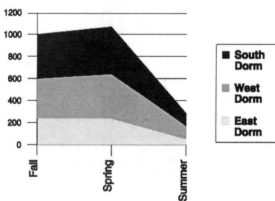

Figure 3.8 Stacked area chart

Distortion. There are several types of distortion commonly found in charts and graphs. As you look, ask the following questions:

♦   Is the baseline (the bottom of the scale) cut off? The cut-off baseline is one of the most common distortions. It focuses the eye on the relevant portion of the data, and is cheaper to produce because the graphic is smaller. But it exaggerates small changes.

44

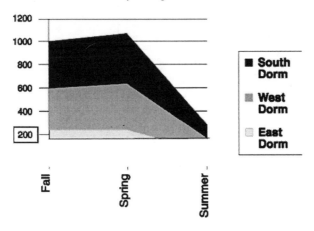

Figure 3.9 Cut-off baseline exaggerates the decline

- Is one dimension elongated or squeezed together? Showing many small changes at frequent intervals, stretched out visually to look like a longer period, will also exaggerate the change.

- Is there enough context given? In particular, are too few data points shown for accurate understanding?

- Do the areas shown exaggerate the true amounts? According to Edward R. Tufte, "the size of effect shown in graphic" must equal the "size of effect shown in data."[6] Here's a common source of distortion:

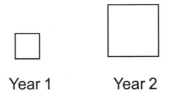

Year 1   Year 2

Figure 3.10 Distortion by area

Say Year 2's growth is twice that of Year 1. Year 2 is shown exactly twice as tall as Year 1. But Year 2 is also shown twice as *wide* as Year 1. So Year 2 is *four times* the size—in area—of Year 1. The graphic distorts the true amounts.

A better graphic would be:

45

Figure 3.11 A more accurate portrayal of "twice the growth"

Other questions to ask:

- Does the title overstate the trend of the data?
- Are dollar amounts adjusted for inflation?
- Are items clearly labeled?

Maps

Maps **represent** the landscape and its features. Beyond the road and weather maps of daily life, maps are important tools for conveying complex information to us as educated citizens, voters, and participants in the economy. Like other information graphics, maps are selective and subject to distortion. As you make sense of a map, consider these factors.

What is the scale? Because maps are smaller than the landscape that they represent, they require a **scale**. The scale states how to relate distances on the map to distances on the ground. For example, one inch may represent five miles. A scale may be presented as a ratio, in words, or as a graphic:

Table 3.12 Scale

Scale Type	Example
Ratio	1:10,000 (1 map unit represents 10,000 units on the ground)
Verbal	One centimeter represents 10,000 meters
Graphic	1 mile

46

With ratio and verbal scales, the larger the second number, the smaller the map scale. (Remember that one fourth [1:4] is smaller than one half [1:2].) With graphic scales, the more distance that a unit represents, the smaller the scale. Small-scale maps are less detailed than large-scale maps.

What is the projection? Maps convert the three-dimensional surface of the earth into the two dimensions of a flat plane. To do so, mapmakers use *projection*, especially in creating world maps. Think of a projection as wrapping a flat piece of paper around a transparent globe. A light from within the globe "projects" the shapes of the earth onto the paper. Different projections produce quite different-looking maps, which have different strengths and uses. Some are valued for their accuracy for navigation, like the Mercator projection. Some, like equal-area projections, preserve the relative size of land masses.

What are the symbols? To read a map well, you must understand the graphic symbols of that map. Many of its special symbols—the different lines, grid marks or "ticks," points, icons, labels, and other markings—are interpreted in a map *key* or *legend* on or near the map.

What kind of information does the map offer? Of the many types of maps, the following are commonly found in newspapers, magazines, and reference works.[7] *Surface maps*, such as road maps, show the location of places on the earth's surface: highways, streets, airports, towns, points of interest. *Location maps* show an area featured in a news story, sometimes with a sidebar or highlight box of explanation. *Event maps* follow a sequence of events from place to place, with commentary—such as the path of John F. Kennedy's motorcade in Dallas on the day of his assassination. *Weather maps* show the distribution of temperatures and the weather forecast. *Distribution maps* show the location (or distribution) of features across an area, such as average December temperatures across the U.S., endangered species in a protected wilderness, or natural resources in a state. *Geologic maps* show the strata below the earth's surface while *topographic maps* show visible features of the earth, such as mountains and rivers, often with *contour lines* that show changes in elevation. *Land use maps* show human activity in an area, such as industry, residences, farmland, and parks. *Data maps* show statistical information across an area, such as cancer rates by state.

Sources of distortion and bias. Maps must represent three dimensions on a flat surface, and they must make many details clear in a small space. As a result, all maps distort reality to some degree (Monmonier, *How to Lie* 1). In addition, some subtle distortions will direct viewers toward certain interpretations of the map. Map readers must be alert for these possible distortions. Following are a few examples of common map distortions and their effects.

47

Lack of detail. The smaller the scale, the cruder the map will be and the less detail it will contain. Symbols on small-scale maps are less likely to be placed accurately because they have to be large enough to see; they also tend to obscure features of the map. Maps created for the Web have an additional problem. They need to be relatively small in file size to load quickly. Some small maps on the Web are so limited in their detail that they give readers only the most generic information.

Distorted relationships and emphasis. Particularly in world maps, the projection distorts portions of the earth's areas, angles, gross shapes, distances, or directions. Different projections have different effects on these relationships. The distortions of a particular means of projection can be used to support political arguments. For example, the common Mercator projection, which became a standard schoolroom map in the early 20th century, enlarges areas near the poles—like the far northern countries of Canada and the former Soviet Union. In particular the distorted view of the Soviet Union's size was taken as evidence of its threat to the United States. At the same time, the Mercator projection diminishes the areas around the tropics (Monmonier 95).

Similarly, using Gestalt and perceptual principles, a map's center is its focal point. English-speaking countries like the United States have typically put Greenwich, England, at the center because the prime meridian (0° latitude) runs through Greenwich. However, that placement also makes the countries of the former British Empire quite prominent. The United Kingdom, the United States, and Canada occupy a central zone, while Asia is sometimes divided in half at the left and right edges of the world map—shoved to the margins. In short, different maps have different political implications.

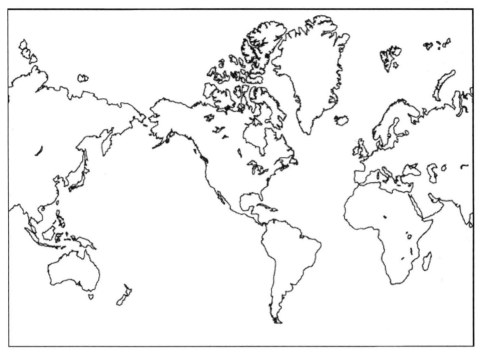

Figure 3.13 Mercator projection with Asia divided

Certain types of maps are prone to specific distortions. ***Data maps*** fill known areas, like states or counties, with points or shading to indicate the density of some statistical feature, like population. These maps are common in news articles. However, readers can too easily focus on the largest geographic areas—or the biggest contrasts in shading—regardless of the numbers involved.

Distortions to persuade. Many maps are created not only to aid viewers' understanding of place relationships, but also to persuade them. For example, subway maps present the subway routes as straight lines. The distances between stops are quite even, like beads on a string. The map eliminates distracting details and shows the routes from the perspective of subway riders (Aziz 53-54). However, the actual routes of the subway, represented on a surface map, twist and turn all over the city that it runs beneath. City subway maps are all based on Henry Beck's 1931 drawing for the London Underground. The clean, modern design and simplicity of the map helped persuade Londoners to accept this new mode of transportation; and so it helped make money for the subway corporation (Forty 237-38).

Maps are constantly used to persuade. Maps of proposed developments are often presented at public meetings and hearings. Like the subway map, their purpose is to persuade officials and the public, so they tend to be highly selective and visually appealing (Monmonier 77-78). Maps may also be used to deny the existence of places or groups of people. Any contested piece of ground is likely to have quite different maps showing the interests of one group rather than another (Monmonier 88-107).

As you look at a map, ask these questions:

- How large an area is shown? How does that fit with other maps of this region?
- What is at the center of the map? What is at the margins?
- How familiar are you with the area covered?
- Do the symbols used have particular connotations—like progress, comfort, security, or (in war zones) aggression?
- Is there a particular interpretation of the map suggested by the title, the caption or explanations, or the symbols used?
- To your knowledge, has anything been omitted?
- Who benefits from the reality shown in this map? Who does not?

As you can see, maps not only convey information, but often a point of view. Some of the same questions useful for analyzing images can be used for maps.

Analyzing information graphics

If you are not used to looking at graphics that contain numbers or complex data, it helps to study a few carefully. Give yourself plenty of time to orient yourself and learn the conventions. (These can differ considerably, especially in scientific and technical fields.) As you become familiar with a certain graphic genre, you will probably need less time to orient yourself, but you will continue to need to study complex displays carefully to understand their points. Not all of the following questions will apply, of course, but many will be relevant.

Rhetorical purpose—information graphics

First consider these questions:

- Where does the graphic appear? Who is the audience?

  The wider the audience, the less complex the graphic is likely to be. It will make a point quickly and may have decorative features for interest. The more specialized the audience, the more complex the graphic may be.

- Who produced it? Do they have any special interest in presenting the information one way or another?

- Does the graphic contain color or visually interesting features? Why do you think that? Relate these to the audience and the ethos of the producers.

- Scan the title above the graphic, and the caption below it, if there is one. Look at the display itself and its labels.

- What type is it—table, bar chart, pie chart, line graph, map?

- What is the general purpose of this type of graphic?

- What is the purpose of this particular display?

- How much time do you think the producers expect viewers to spend looking at it? Why?

- What is the source of the data?

- What clues do you have about the total size of the ***data set***—the body of evidence from which the numbers are drawn—that the display is taken from?

- Examine the display closely: the columns and rows of a table, the lines or bars of a graph, or the spatial organization of a map. Find the baseline or scale.

- Point out the main area of interest. If you are permitted, circle or trace around this area.

- Draw or state the main area's relationship to another part of the graphic.

- Keeping the display's purpose in mind, state what you see portrayed. Write down:
  1. the main point that you take from it,
  2. any subpoints, and
  3. any questions that you have after close examination.

- Do you detect any distortions in the display of the data?

Summary

- *Visual literacy* is the ability to analyze and interpret visuals in our culture. It includes awareness of distorting elements in visuals.

- "Pictures" can be divided into *images*, including news photographs, conceptual photographs, lifelike or stylized drawings, cartoons, clip art, and advertisements; and *information graphics*, including tables, charts, graphs, and maps.

- In making sense of images, consider their rhetorical purpose, the overall design, the people depicted, the setting, the use or absence of color, the text, and the story told, including whose story is told by the image and whose is excluded.

- In making sense of information graphics, consider their rhetorical purpose, the general type, and the particular features. State the graphic's point in your own words. Check for common sources of distortion.

Exercises

1. Examine a news photograph, ad, or other image from a magazine using the questions for image analysis. Bring a copy of the image to discuss with other class members.

2. Look at the drawing of hands below, an image that is typical of business clip art. Using the questions for image analysis, what can you say about this image?

3. Compare an information graphic from a daily newspaper or weekly news magazine with one from a more specialized publication, such as *Scientific American*. How would you characterize the differences? What reasons can you give for those differences?

4. Analyze maps used as illustrations. (For example, see the cover of this textbook. Some editions use a map as a background.)

5. If your library carries English-language newspapers from other countries, examine the location maps that accompany their articles. Find a map of the same area in your hometown, regional, or national newspaper. Are there any differences of emphasis or features?

6. What types of graphs and charts are you expected to interpret in your classes? What pointers have you found helpful in making sense of these displays?

Notes

[1]That division is a result of centuries of Western literacy based on a phonetic writing system, plus printing press technology. See Bolter, pp. 59-60.

[2]Ellen Lupton and J. Abbott Miller analyze stock photography in "Pictures for Rent," in *Design Writing Research: Writing on Graphic Design* (New York: Kiosk-Princeton Architectural, 1996), 121-34.

[3]These questions combine rhetorical, aesthetic, semiotic, and ideological analysis. They are based on Molly Bang, *Picture This: Perception and Composition* (Boston: Bulfinch-Little, Brown, 1991); Arthur Asa Berger, "Sex and Symbol in Fashion Advertising and Analyzing Signs and Systems," in Diana George and John Trimbur, *Reading Culture: Contexts for Critical Reading and Writing*, 3rd ed. (New York: Longman, 1999), pp. 186-93; Gunther Kress and Theo van Leeuwen, *Reading Images: The Grammar of Visual Design* (London: Routledge, 1996); and Gail E. Hawisher and Cynthia L. Selfe, *Literacy, Technology, and Society: Confronting the Issues* (Upper Saddle River, NJ: Prentice-Hall, 1997), p. 580. See Chapter 9 for explanations of aesthetics (chiefly modernism), semiotics, and ideological criticism.

[4]Journalism uses the term ***information graphics*** while the sciences tend to use ***data graphics*** or ***data displays***. This discussion omits several other types of graphics and displays, such as scientific and technical illustrations, diagrams, flowcharts, blueprints, and architectural drawings.

[5]The terms are used interchangeably here.

⁶Visual Display, p. 57. For more about Tufte's theories of information graphics, see Chapter 9.

⁷Adapted from Finberg and Itule, pp. 163-66.

CHAPTER 4

Planning Visual Design

As you plan a document, consider its visual design as part of the rhetorical process of analyzing your readers. The better you can imagine your readers as they read, the better you will be able to design a document so that they can read and act. This chapter presents an overall strategy for planning visual design, then applies that strategy to a variety of genres.

Consider genres, purposes, readers, and contexts together. The next pages contain many detailed issues to consider, as well as planning worksheets. As you answer questions and fill in blanks, remember that readers read in specific situations for specific reasons. That means that their needs can change. Therefore, do not isolate one answer from another. For example, if your readers are well educated but in a hurry, able only to scan your document at this point, then you need to take both considerations into account in the visual design. That is, your readers may be able to read dense paragraphs of text, but in this document, they will truly appreciate an attractive, accessible, visually organized design with headings and an overview.

What is your document's purpose?

Your purpose in writing is a major factor in planning for its look and visual features. We have defined **genre** as one means of defining rhetorical purpose and action. Later in this chapter, specific genres will be analyzed. Here are some additional aspects of purpose to consider.

Rhetorical appeal. In what ways does your document rely on logos, ethos, and pathos? Visual design always contributes to ethos, as we saw in Chapter 1. It can also organize, contributing to logos. Images and other visual features may contribute to pathos, an appeal to readers' feelings.

Relationship with readers. What do you want the document to do? Another way to state that is: What relationship do you want to establish with readers? In the terms of James Britton and his co-researchers, these relationships may be *expressive*, *transactional*, or *poetic* (88-90). You may want readers to:

◆ Share your personal values, opinions, and interests—an *expressive* purpose.

- Act on your information and claims: reply to you, argue with you, find out more information, plan another action (such as making an appointment with an official or a clinic or approving your request)—a ***transactional*** purpose.

- Engage with you in a playful or aesthetic experience—a ***poetic*** or artistic purpose.

The images and type to convey the experience of a favorite poem will be very different from the design of a fact sheet comparing the advantages and disadvantages of recycling methods. Many documents also combine rhetorical purposes. Most documents have at least some expressive purpose because we all want to be thought well of, yet a particular document may be primarily transactional.

Flexibility of genre. As explained in Chapter 2, some genres have strict format rules while others offer greater freedom. More flexibility gives you more choices for a document's look, but may also require more attention to and planning of the design.

Lifespan. We all like to think of our writing as timeless, but in fact documents often have specific lifespans. A resume is usually up to date for a few months, at most a year or two. A proposal may serve its purpose in a matter of weeks. A flyer may fulfill its destiny inside a week. As you plan visuals, consider the length of time that you expect a document to be effective.

Publication method and copies. How will you convey your document to readers? Is your document a unique item, such as a portfolio, memoir, or academic paper? Or is it intended to be reproduced in many copies, such as a brochure, newsletter, or flyer? Will it be projected on a screen or published on the Web? While these questions concern production, they relate closely to your ultimate purpose of delivering the document and the type of visuals that you can reasonably produce—and reproduce.

Significance. Evaluate each aspect of visual design against its significance for the document. Ask yourself what the success of this document means. A job? A large percentage of your course grade? Approval for a community project? The reputation of an organization? In that case, spending time, money, and effort for the best document design and visuals is probably justified. If you are producing the final document yourself, you will have the benefit of learning a great deal as well. However, you may be able to get similar results more quickly or cheaply, or with fewer facilities, than you had originally planned. For example, if you are explaining the techniques of mountain rescue, a hand-drawn sketch of a belay mechanism, carefully labeled, can be more effective than an inept computer-generated illustration or even a photograph. If time is critical, as in creating a flyer to be posted for a meeting, then you will probably need to do the best design that you can produce and copy quickly. Weigh significance with the factors discussed in the section on facilities.

Who are your readers?

Just as with your words, your visual communication requires analysis of your readers and their goals. Consider these issues:

Number. The number of readers is one factor in deciding what design resources might be appropriate. In general, the more readers your document will have, the more time, money, and people may reasonably be devoted to designing the project. However, the importance of some documents that have only a few readers—proposals, resumes, portfolios—may also justify time and expense in design and printing costs.

Age and range of ages. Age affects both genre expectations and visual acuity. Readers over 50 years old may not be able to read small type. College-age readers may expect a high level of visual design in documents intended to appeal to them as a group. High-school students are also sophisticated consumers of graphics. They readily interpret the quality and relevance of visuals and relate those to the author's view of teenagers and their interests (Schriver 171).

Education. Readers with college or postgraduate education are used to reading long texts without much visual information. However, depending on other circumstances, they may actually prefer more visually-informative texts. Documents to reach people who have less formal schooling or who do not read much need special attention to visual design. In particular, they need accessible, visually organized text rather than dense paragraphs. Simply increasing the ratio of pictures to text may not address these readers' needs. Researching their needs is important. If your document will reach readers of varying levels of education, you may plan a design that is attractive and accessible in several ways at once.

Job background. Readers with backgrounds in or strongly influenced by the professional cultures of science, technology, or business may expect considerable quantitative information in charts and graphs. They may correspondingly prefer less text. Readers in the humanities tend to prefer text as the focus. Readers with arts backgrounds will be attentive to the overall aesthetics of the document. Some readers may object to any visual element that is not covered by the genre expectations of their field. Adding an image to the title page of your academic paper, for example, may be considered inappropriate. Remember that your instructor is also a primary reader.

Gender, race, class. As we saw in Chapter 3, there may be hidden biases of gender, race, class, and culture in many visuals. Be sensitive to these as you choose clip art, photographs, or other representational images for your document. If you cannot obtain images of people that show diversity and equal participation, you may decide to use non-representational (abstract) images or focus on objects rather than people. Many newsletter editors and designers have faced this dilemma. In addition, class may be a consideration in the overall approach to visuals and the proportion of visuals to text.

Culture. Many other cultural factors may influence readers' visual expectations. Europeans use standard paper sizes different from those usually available in the United States. Likewise, in Europe it is more common to use sans serif typefaces for lengthy texts while in the United States serif typefaces (like this one, Garamond BookCondensed) remain the rule for long texts. Cultural norms may also influence the number and kinds of illustrations that readers prefer and respond to. Strict adherents of Islam regard pictures (representational images of any type) as blasphemous, while abstract images are acceptable. Various cultures treat the meaning and symbolism of common colors like red quite differently (Coe 150, 320). Again, asking for reader input about preferences—i.e., user testing—can help.

As we saw with the Army maintenance manual in Chapter 3, it can be difficult to make visual choices to appeal to a group of readers yet not exclude other readers who have good reason to view the document.

Familiarity with similar documents. Knowledge of similar documents—genre knowledge—helps readers anticipate and make use of the visual design. For example, knowing that a scientific article typically has an abstract and then is arranged into sections with headings for Introduction, Methods, Results, and Discussion (called IMRAD structure) enables readers familiar with these articles to locate and evaluate information quickly. In fact, readers of scientific articles often read the Discussion before they read the Methods sections. An article that does not follow the expected format will possibly confuse and frustrate the reader. On the other hand, a fresh approach to a familiar genre, such as a brochure, may awaken interest in readers jaded by the usual—as long as they are convinced it is still a brochure and can find what they need from it.

Knowledge of a genre's visual cues may also be used to select and disregard documents. Readers often encounter hundreds, even thousands, of examples of certain genres. If their reading is voluntary, they may use visual design to classify a document and then disregard it. Chapter 2 mentions junk mail in this regard. Another example: many college bulletin boards are crowded with flyers. Potential readers may notice the flyers and correctly understand their genre, but decide not to pay attention to any one of them. Their decision may change, of course, as when a student or faculty member waits outside a classroom and reads a bulletin board to pass the time.

Reading goals. Will readers be primarily scanning or skimming to get the gist of the document? Will they need to search for specific items, such as a particular model of a product? Are they going to settle in to read receptively or critically? See Chapter 2 for a fuller explanation of these goals.

Setting for reading. Documents not only compete with other documents for readers' attention, but also compete with the overall setting and tasks unrelated to reading. For example, as a class project, a group of students planned to create health information materials for state transportation workers. One item that the students planned was a visually attractive poster to put in the workers' break room. After interviewing several workers, however, the students decided against the poster. Although the break room had tables, employees spent very little time there, usually just enough to get refreshments from the vending machines.[1] Instead of a poster, the students created small flyers and brochures that workers could voluntarily pick up with their paychecks. As you plan a document, consider where readers will encounter it and what interferes with their attention to it: poor lighting, glare, wind or rain (if outdoors), noise, distance from which it must be read, lack of seating or reading surfaces, preoccupation with other tasks, and the like.

In general, the more that reading requires a voluntary decision to get the document, and the more competition and distractions that readers may have in first approaching your document, the more that first impressions—including visual impression—matter for them. Otherwise, they will not even pick it up.

What resources do you have?

Knowing your purpose and readers, you must decide how you will produce this document. That is, you need to assess your resources. These include the talent and experience of the people involved, the production facilities that you have available, and the time and money you have. All of these must be weighed against the significance of the project. Because they tend to require an approach to production that is somewhat different from text, visuals usually add time and complexity to a document project. Planning and flexibility are key.

People. First consider who will be involved, what they are good at, and what they are willing or able to learn, given the purpose, time, and scope of the project. If you will be the sole producer—

researcher, writer, graphic designer, and publisher—consider what you already know how to do and what you may need to learn. Whether you are working alone or in a team, line up resource people to ask questions of. These may be your instructor, lab assistants, librarians, or other students.

Facilities. Do you or your group intend to produce this document yourselves? If so, what facilities do you have? If you plan to use computers, are you aware of what software you have available and whether it can produce the visuals that you want? The same is true of publication—if you plan to print the document, what printing facilities do you have? Are they compatible with your computer and software? Do they support color and intensive graphics (which may take a good deal of printer memory)? Do you know what file formats are used? If you plan to present the document electronically—as a Web site, e-mail message, slide presentation, floppy disk, CD-ROM—is the presentation setup compatible with your production facilities?

It is not necessary to have a computer to produce good visuals. Pencil, pen, and ruler still yield good results for charts, graphs, and line drawings. Felt markers are effective for creating small areas of color, especially if you are using color to cue the reader to related items. For portfolios, colored construction paper, cutouts from magazines (not library copies!), scissors, and rubber cement can be used to create title and section pages. However, depending on campus resources, your instructor may expect you to employ specific software as part of your project.

Time. For any project that incorporates document design or visuals, starting early is important. If you intend to have charts that rely on data, you need to gather the data. The same computer software that has put visual communication within reach for many college writers also places a burden on them. Learning new software can take time, lots of time. That is especially true of page layout, graphic editing, and many Web authoring programs. Even simple "paint" software can be difficult and frustrating to the newcomer. Good planning worksheets can help you. For an example, see the end guide at of this chapter.

Money. Some types of documents may incur costs. For example, you may want to print resumes on "rag" paper or brochures on heavy or colored paper, an additional expense. You may need to have photographs developed or slide transparencies produced at a print or copy shop. You may need to pay a fee to use certain copyrighted materials. If you decide on professional printing for a brochure or newsletter, the costs may be much higher than you expected. Be sure to get an estimate early in your project, giving the printer details about the visual features—color, layout, and the like. The rule: color is free on the screen, but usually costly on the printed page.

People revisited—asking readers for input. One of the best ways to find out how readers actually approach a document is to ask them. In technical writing and interface design, where print and electronic documents may reach thousands of readers, this process has come to be called field testing or **usability testing**. Involving readers in the planning of your document can help you with ideas for the visual design, the information to include or exclude, and the argument and arrangement. Their experience can be invaluable. As the students found in interviewing the transportation workers, there is no substitute for reader input. Some documents are designed for a particular decision-maker or client. Checking with your client about preferences for format and visuals is a good idea. If you are unsure if having readers review your work is suitable for your task, ask your instructor. In general, testing your document and revising it based on reader input is not only smart, but also ethical. It shows responsibility to your readers.

Giving credit. Creating and using visuals often involves the work of others. Acknowledge your sources and the people who have assisted you. Put a credit line below illustrations and images (particularly in academic papers and proposals). In other documents, it is proper to give a list of credits for design and graphics work, as well as writing and editing, in a separate section called "Acknowledgments" or, in newsletters, a masthead.

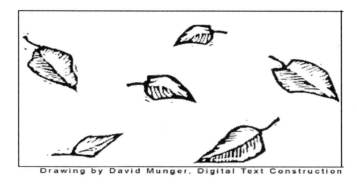

Drawing by David Munger, Digital Text Construction

Figure 4.1 Sample credit line

How do you turn analysis into visual features?

You have analyzed your purpose, readers, and resources. You've contacted a few of the people who are likely readers of your document. Now what? The following sections suggest how a rhetorical analysis of typical genres can be translated into design features. As you consider these, realize that design choices both empower and limit. Each choice is a tradeoff. For example, deciding to keep a fact sheet to one page limits the information, but may increase its attractiveness to the intended readers.

Single-panel genres

These are the genres that readers generally see "all at once": poems, logos, resumes, flyers, and posters. These genres may have complex visual structures, but readers usually do not need special navigational features as they read.

Setting for a poem, quotation, or graffiti

Purpose: Expressive and artistic, to establish a relationship with readers and invite them to engage in a many-faceted understanding of the words presented
Rhetorical appeals: Ethos and pathos, logos
Copies: One or very few—representing a unique experience
Lifespan: Probably more than a year
Readers: This document may appeal across ages and backgrounds, though cultural, educational, and linguistic differences may be important
Setting: Indoors, normal reading distance, seated
Distraction: Little
Reading goals: Receptive understanding, voluntarily undertaken—not evaluative
Reader's immediate action: Reflection, imaginative participation
Format: One page or screen, sometimes more
Visual flexibility: Great
Visual/text ratio: Either visuals or text may predominate

Visual features. The great visual flexibility of genre offers an opportunity to learn about visual design and its impact. To create an experience that parallels or contrasts with your understanding of the words, you can employ the whole range of visual design: type, layout, and illustrations. You can also call on all the symbolic and associative elements of visual design.

TIPS for setting poems, quotations, and graffiti

◆ Much of the page or screen can be illustration or framing space.
◆ If you use multiple panels, you can tell a visual story or use color, metaphor, repeated items or other grouping strategies to lead readers among the panels.

Resume

Purpose: Transactional, to get an interview for a job or for entrance to a special academic program.
Rhetorical appeals: Ethos and logos
Copies: Many
Lifespan: Medium to long—several months to more than a year
Readers: Targeted to prospective employers or faculty admissions committees
Setting: Seated indoors, normal reading distance
Distractions: Time pressure to complete task, competition from other work
Reading goals: Skimming and scanning at first, then evaluative; reading not voluntary; other resumes compete directly for readers' attention
Reader's immediate action: Reject, call for interview, or set aside for further action (filing, further evaluation)
Format: For college students, usually one printed page
Visual flexibility: Limited but by no means rigid
Visual/text ratio: Text well balanced by visual ordering, white space

Visual features. Resumes must fit the many conventions of this genre, yet there is more freedom than you may imagine. E-mail and scannable resumes impose more limits to design. To create a clear organization and enhance your credibility, visual information and text must be balanced. There should be neither too much white space nor too much text. For example, one human resources director at a large company first gives a resume a 5-second "squint" test to see if the page is full enough but not overcrowded. He tends to judge skimpy resumes as deficient or lacking, while over-full pages offend his sense of propriety and design. If these judgments seem harsh, they are by no means unique. Because readers scan resumes quickly, the key to the design of a printed resume is a clear visual hierarchy of information to aid this scanning and accurate evaluation. Use gestalt principles of grouping and proximity to help readers, and avoid visual devices that impair legibility.

TIPS for print resumes

- Provide a clear visual hierarchy of information to aid quick scanning and accurate evaluation.
- Put your name at the top in the largest size or heaviest weight of type, and make headings the next largest size or weight—and so on.
- Don't let headings "hang" between blocks of info—put them closer to the sections they introduce and farther from the previous section.
- Be consistent in your use of visual emphasis—bold, caps, and the like.

- Use bold rather than underlining.
- Use all caps (uppercase letters) and italics for short stretches only.
- Make key contact information, such as phone number(s), address, and e-mail address, large enough to see and accessible—near the top, not the bottom where it could be missed by eyes, scanner, or fax machine.
- If possible, laser-print your resume or have it professionally printed.

Increasingly prospective employers are asking for e-mail or scannable resumes. Print resumes, skimmed by human eyes, benefit from the clear visual formatting mentioned earlier. However, many e-mail systems do not support that kind of formatting. What results is a hash of extra characters and information that makes the resume useless. E-mail resumes, therefore, must be sent as plain "ASCII" text. They may still benefit from the limited formatting options that cue the reader to main sections and group-related items.

CHRIS TOMAS

150 Pendleton Avenue
Central, SC 29333
(864) 555-3582

TOMAS@CLEMSON.EDU
http://people.clemson.edu/~tomar/

OBJECTIVE

Internship in law firm

EDUCATION

Clemson University
B.S., Sociology, expected May 2004
Minors: Management, History

RELATED COURSEWORK

Legal Environment of Business
Race, Gender, Class
Business Writing
Advanced Expository Writing

WORK EXPERIENCE

CLEMSON UNIVERSITY, Clemson, SC
2001-present
Part-Time Work-Study Assistant, Access and Equities Office. Answer phone, schedule appointments, prepare mailings. Assist students by making available information regarding ADA (Americans with Disabilities Act) and state access and equity laws. Responsible for desktop publishing campus handbook on resources for students with disabilities. Edited copy for the handbook and presented to supervisor for approval.

GENERAL STORES, Greenville, SC
Summers 1998-2001
Sales Associate, Hardware. Assist customers in purchasing decisions and transactions. Demonstrate process of remodelling kitchens using interior design computer software. Train new associates.

OTHER SKILLS

Microsoft Word, PowerPoint, Excel and Publisher; HomePro design software
Excellent writing, copyediting, and research skills
Basic carpentry

VOLUNTEER SERVICE

Habitat for Humanity, 1998-present

References available upon request

Figure 4.2 A print resume format

65

- Put your resume directly into the body of the e-mail message.
- Place all text flush left (against the left margin).
- Make all text the same size.
- Use no formatting—no bold, italics, or underlining.
- For headings use all caps (uppercase).
- Separate main sections by vertical spaces (press "Enter").
- Be consistent in spacing.
- Avoid tabs, tables, and columns.

Furthermore, large employers that receive many resumes often scan paper resumes by computer and then electronically search the results for keywords. Only resumes that survive the scanning and search processes are actually read. Your resume is scanned as an image, literally a picture, that is then interpreted into letters and text through OCR (Optical Character Recognition) software. Your main goal is to create a clear image so that the software recognizes every letter.

In sum, you may need to prepare more than one version of your resume with these different visual formats in mind.

TIPS for scannable resumes

- Use white or light 8.5" x 11" paper, printed on one side only.
- Avoid paper with a patterned background or heavy "watermark," and print in black only.
- Laser-print the resume if possible.
- Avoid dot matrix or other printing of poor quality.
- Send originals, not copies.
- Do not fold or staple.
- Use standard typefaces like Times, Arial, Helvetica, Century Schoolbook.
- Make type size 10 to 14 points.
- As long as the letters do not touch each other, you may use bold or all caps for headings.
- Avoid italics, underlining, script, shading, and other special formatting.
- Do not condense the type or the space between lines.
- Avoid columns or rules (long horizontal or vertical lines).
- Use a standard resume layout.

◆ Use key words to describe your skills, especially those phrases used in your field.

```
CHRIS TOMAS

150 Pendleton Avenue
Central, SC 29333
(864) 555-3582
ctomas@clemson.edu


OBJECTIVE

Internship in law firm


EDUCATION

Clemson University
B.S., Sociology, expected May 2004
Minors: Management, History


RELATED COURSEWORK

Legal Environment of Business
Race, Gender, Class
Business Writing
Advanced Expository Writing


WORK EXPERIENCE

CLEMSON UNIVERSITY, Clemson, SC
2001-present
Part-Time Work-Study Assistant, Access and Equities Office. Answer phone, schedule
appointments, prepare mailings. Assist students by making available information
regarding ADA (Americans with Disabilities Act) and state access and equity laws.
Responsible for desktop publishing campus handbook on resources for students with
disabilities. Edited copy for the handbook and presented to supervisor for approval.

GENERAL STORES, Greenville, SC
Summers 1998-2001
Sales Associate, Hardware. Assist customers in purchasing decisions and transac-
tions. Demonstrate process of remodelling kitchens using interior design computer
software. Train new associates.


OTHER SKILLS

Microsoft Word, PowerPoint, Excel and Publisher; HomePro design software
Excellent writing, copyediting, and research skills
Basic carpentry


VOLUNTEER SERVICE

Habitat for Humanity, 1998-present


REFERENCES AVAILABLE UPON REQUEST
```

Figure 4.3 An e-mail or scannable resume format

67

Flyer

Purpose: Transactional but also expressive (and possibly artistic), to publicize a meeting, event, activity, or opportunity

Rhetorical appeal: Ethos, pathos, and logos

Copies: Many

Lifespan: Short—days or weeks

Readers: Wide range of passersby, targeting one or more subgroups who may need or want to know about the occasion—analyze the characteristics of your audience closely for this genre

Setting: Indoors on bulletin boards or outdoors on kiosks, first viewing distance 10-15 feet, then closer for reading

Distractions: Crowds, poor lighting, other goals, lack of time

Reading goals: Skimming, then scanning; reading is voluntary; other flyers compete directly for readers' attention

Reader's immediate action: Decide to remember the event or not, note specific info mentally or in writing

Format: One page

Visual flexibility: Considerable freedom

Visual/text ratio: Lots of white space and visuals to text

Visual features. To attract and interest readers sated with other similar documents, a flyer needs good visibility to viewers approaching from 10-15 feet away plus bold design—layout, typography, possibly images—in keeping with the ethos of the event. Critical information should be clearly grouped. Flyers may need lamination for extended outdoor use or tear-offs that help readers recall info. In general, avoid visuals that require careful reading or interpretation, such as charts or tables.

TIPS for flyers

- Use large type that has good legibility and weight, that is, fairly thick strokes.
- Group information clearly, "framing" it with ample white space.
- To add impact, use bold design, clip art, or decorative visuals in keeping with the ethos of the event.

Speech Communication Majors

"Powerful Non-Defensive Communication"

Please attend TODAY'S presentation
by Sharon Ellison,
Consultant/Author

Wednesday, 4:00 – 5:30, November 4
111 Lee Hall Auditorium

Extra Credit ?

Note: Check with your S&CS faculty to see if this will count
as EXTRA CREDIT. If not, just go. It's a GREAT
presentation!

Figure 4.4 Sample flyer by Amy Bumgarner

Fact sheet

Purpose: Transactional, to explain key points about an issue, an organization, or a program
Rhetorical appeals: Logos, ethos
Copies: Many
Lifespan: Medium to long—months to more than a year
Readers: People who already have some interest, such as the audience for a meeting, or members of a group who receive a mailing
Setting: Sitting indoors at a meeting or opening mail at home or office, normal reading distance
Distractions: In a meeting, the noise of discussion or lecture; at home or work, the needs of others, phone, television or radio, pressing tasks
Reading goals: Skimming or scanning, then searching and possibly reading entire document for critical comprehension; reading is voluntary; other documents may compete for readers' attention
Reader's immediate action: Be motivated to cast a vote, call to enroll in a program, buy a product or service, or contact the organization or other people to discuss the issue
Format: Typically one page, or one sheet printed front and back
Visual flexibility: Considerable freedom of layout
Visual/text ratio: Text may predominate, but spacing and visual layering enable readers to search quickly for needed information

Visual features. To organize complex information and make it attractive, in keeping with the sponsoring group's ethos, use chunking, layering, visual hierarchy. To attract and interest readers who may be apprehensive about the issue or the complexity of the information, you may need to incorporate other visuals, such as images, tables, or clear graphics.

TIPS for fact sheets

- Lead readers into the issues with bold or highlighted headings, and, if appropriate, drawings or photographs.
- Chunk information into short paragraphs.
- Create clear tables for comparison of data and options.
- Use vivid, simple bar charts and other easily interpreted information graphics. Keep numerical data simple and explain it well.
- Put contact information in a separate section, visually identified.
- Ask for reader input.

Logo

Purpose: Expressive, artistic, to establish and maintain a visual identity with viewers and readers
Rhetorical appeal: Ethos, pathos
Copies: Many
Lifespan: Long—months or years
Readers: Wide range—even those who don't read a particular document will look at the logo
Setting: Indoors, viewing at arm's length while reading organization's letters, memos, or Web site; outdoors on flyers
Reading goals: Skimming and scanning
Reader's immediate action: Form a favorable impression of the organization and perhaps gain a sense of its mission
Format: Usually a computer image file that can be copied, resized, and placed on a variety of print and screen documents
Visual flexibility: Considerable freedom, but constrained by group ethos
Visual/text ratio: Visual predominates; text elements, such as name or initials, are treated as design features but must remain legible

Visual features. To convey the ethos of the organization visually, in a means acceptable to members of the organization, as well as to send a clear message to readers, logos need to be simple and distinctive. They are often combined with the name of the group (these designs are then called **logotypes**), so they need to be coordinated with the typography of the letterhead. Because they are resized and used on both paper and screens, they tend to need bold elements that weather the degradation of different media and browsers. Likewise, they must be clear in black and white as well as color. Logos convey stability, so a design everyone can live with is key. Testing with members and potential readers is of great importance. Also try the logo in different sizes and formats. Because they are widely distributed and present a group's ethos, logos can be one of the most difficult types of design ("A Raven" 50).

TIPS for logos

- Gather input from the group or client before you design: What ethos does the group want to convey to readers? What do members want to avoid? On what materials will the logo appear?
- Do preliminary sketches (thumbnails), and share them with the group for more input.
- See how the logo looks in black and white as well as color.
- Print or reproduce the logo in several sizes to ensure its clarity.

* Test it on group members and others outside the group. What sense of the group do they get from this design?

Poster

Purpose: Transactional, to explain an activity or research study; or transactional and expressive, to promote an organization or issue
Rhetorical appeal: Logos, ethos
Copies: One—unique
Lifespan: Results of research studies—very short (one or two meetings). Posters for information fairs and meetings—short to long (one meeting, or several meetings over a year or two)
Readers: Conference or meeting participants who already have an interest in the general area. Get information about your specific audience.
Setting: Indoors on foot; first viewing distance approximately 10 feet, then somewhat closer (3-6 feet) for reading
Distractions and special constraints: Reading while standing, possibly with other people obscuring sections of the poster; competition from nearby posters
Reading goals: Skimming and scanning, then searching, receptive reading; possibly evaluation; reading is voluntary
Reader's immediate action: Ask questions of presenter. For research studies, evaluate initial importance of information and compare mentally with other studies; for organizational posters, gain a sense of group's mission and key activities
Format: Text and graphics pages fastened to standard poster board or foam board, or to a fixed display background
Visual flexibility: Considerable freedom, but constraints by field, especially for research posters
Visual/text ratio: The text elements are important, but the visual usually predominates (Day 149)

Visual features. Poster presentations, or simply posters, are a specialized genre for conventions, meetings, and information fairs. The posters are propped on tables or mounted on stands at eye level. To attract readers to the poster from 8-10 feet away, large clear titles and attractive layout are important. To explain complex information to these readers on foot, posters need a transparently clear organization. If the sequence of information is important, they may need navigational signals such as numbers or arrows. Visual elements such as medium to large illustrations, graphs, and tables balance or even predominate over text. Scientific research posters follow the IMRAD sequence—Introduction, Methods, Results, and Discussion (Day 149). The pages of text and visuals are typically in columns that read top to bottom and left to right (Penrose and Katz 112). Tables and diagrams or graphs with clear, large lettering help scientific readers take in data. For information fair posters, there is more freedom of layout. Large photographs and other kinds of images can play a role. For both types, color can help to attract and organize readers' experience of the poster. Good contrast between major elements and clear, consistent groupings—that is, clear from a distance of 3-6 feet—are key.

TIPS for posters

- Storyboard your presentation, paying careful attention to the selection and sequencing of information.
- If the type of poster backing is not specified, use standard foam board, which is more rigid than cardboard. Sizes range from 20" x 30" to 40" x 60". Attach computer-printed pages of text and graphics with rubber cement or special adhesive.
- Use 1-inch (72-point) high letters for the main title and important information such as the organization or your names as authors (scientific presentations). You may buy press-on vinyl or transfer lettering, or produce these in word processing, presentation, or graphics programs.
- Use 24-point type for the text (Day 150).
- For legibility, be sure that the titles, text, and visuals contrast well with the background.
- Break up long text passages into shorter, chunked paragraphs and bulleted lists.

For scientific or technical presentations:

- Check with the meeting organizers for size and format requirements.
- Arrange pages of text and graphics in columns, placing the introduction at the top left and ending with the conclusions at the bottom right of the poster.
- Create informative graphics such as tables, graphs, or technical illustrations and label them clearly. These graphics can be more complex and quantitative than those for oral presentations, as viewers can take as much time reading as they wish.
- Use color to attract interest, cue navigation, and distinguish important features in tables and graphics.
- Include a list of works cited.

For information fairs:

- Design a colorful poster that will appeal to the audience you hope to reach.
- Use the range of visuals that appeal to your viewers: photographs, brightly colored images,

and decorative details in addition to information graphics. Simplified tables and charts appeal to a wide audience.

* Use bold graphics—lettering may be large, the design daring—to convey your organization's message and identity.

* Show cultural, gender, and racial sensitivity in choices of illustration.

* Test your design storyboard and visual choices with a few intended viewers.

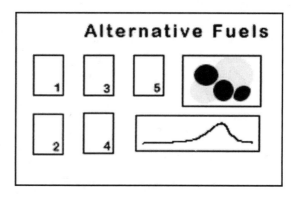

Figure 4.5 A poster presentation

Multi-panel genres

These are the genres in which readers must turn pages, open folded sections, scroll through screens, click on hyperlinks, or simply wait to see all of the document: academic papers, reports, proposals, brochures, newsletters, slide presentations, Web sites, portfolios. Of necessity, they unfold through time. In addition to other visual elements, all of these genres require close attention to visual organization and navigation through the document (see, for example, Figures 8.16-8.18).

Academic paper and report

Purpose: Transactional, to convince reader of writer's knowledge and control of a subject
Rhetorical appeal: Logos, ethos
Copies: One for each decision-maker
Lifespan: Short to medium—a few weeks or months
Readers: Supervisors, teachers, or sponsors, all of whom already have some knowledge and interest in the general area

Setting: Sitting indoors, normal reading distance

Distractions and constraints: Time pressure, competition from other tasks and documents, including other papers and reports

Reading goals: Skimming, scanning; then receptive and evaluative reading

Order of reading: Typical busy readers first read the title, then the abstract or summary (if any), then the headings and captions for visuals, the first and last pages of chapters or sections, and the opening sentences of paragraphs (Killingsworth and Palmer 262-63)

Reader's immediate action: Evaluate overall worth of report; ask for clarification, expansion or revision.

Format: Several typed or printed pages, possibly bound in a report cover or notebook

Visual flexibility: Likely to be quite limited.

Visual/text ratio: Text elements significant, but clear visual organization and well-chosen supporting data graphics may weigh as much as text for some readers

Visual features. In many respects, reports have the rigidity of academic papers, so find out requirements well ahead of planning and producing visuals. The following tips are based on general document design guidelines for informal reports. Clear attention to visual organization and visual hierarchy of information—chunking and layering—assists busy readers in scanning and searching for pertinent information. You can see that readers' scanning is reflected in their typical order of reading. Ample margins look good and invite readers to make notes. Tables and graphs summarize and emphasize data, enabling readers quickly to make comparisons and determine trends. Navigation is handled by standard visual sequencing methods for academic and business documents: clear title and headings, plus page numbers, captions, and callouts. Long reports should also have a table of contents, an abstract or executive summary, and appendices for additional data. Running heads can also help.

> **NOTE:** For more information on the design of academic research papers and formal reports, see a style manual such as the *MLA Handbook* or the *Publication Manual of the American Psychological Association*. A business or technical writing textbook is another good resource.

TIPS for academic papers and reports

- Find out any requirements for the paper or report's format and visuals.
- Give the document an informative title.
- Number the pages.
- Divide a **report** into sections with informative headings.

- Do not divide an academic **paper** into sections unless your format so allows.
- If you argue from or report on quantitative information, include appropriate tables, charts, or graphs. Label them clearly and consistently.
- If you are explaining complex objects, events, or processes, consider images—diagrams, maps, drawings, photos—as part of your logical appeal.
- Unless your format specifies otherwise, place the visual close to the point where you refer to it in the text.
- In the text, make a point about each visual included.
- Refer to each visual clearly through a callout: "The following table shows ___." "In Figure 2, _____."
- If you copy or adapt a visual from another source, such as the Web, give credit in a source line below the visual.

Proposal

Purpose: Transactional, to gain approval or funding of an activity or project
Rhetorical appeal: Logos, ethos, and pathos in appealing to those in need who will benefit
Copies: One for each decision-maker
Lifespan: Short to medium—a few weeks or months
Readers: As with reports, supervisors, teachers, or sponsors—plus community leaders
Setting: Sitting indoors, normal reading distance
Distractions and constraints: Time pressure, competition from other tasks and documents, including other proposals
Reading goals: Skimming, scanning; then receptive and evaluative reading; searching for important specific facts
Order of reading: Same order as reports, keying on the title, then the abstract or summary (if any), then the headings and captions for visuals
Reader's immediate action: Evaluate overall worth of proposal; ask for clarification, expansion or revision; decide to approve or fund
Format: Several typed or printed pages, possibly bound in a report cover or notebook
Visual flexibility: Major parts of proposal fairly constrained but some freedom
Visual/text ratio: Text elements most significant but visual design important for first impression and clear access, graphics important for argument

Visual features. Proposals may seem like reports, but there is a difference. Proposals present new ideas for action and may also form the basis of partnerships to create change, so they need to make a good first impression. Good visual design supports the ethos of the requesting person or group and shows a commitment to the project. Typefaces, graphical elements, and any images used should first convey the seriousness and professionalism of the proposal writer(s). The same clear visual organization that you employ in reports is also appropriate in proposals. Yet many proposals can also use some visual innovation. The spirit of the proposed project can be conveyed in a well-chosen image or photograph, especially if it shows who or what will benefit from the project. For example, a cropped photograph of the entrance to a clinic, showing the name of the facility and its director standing outside, may accompany a proposal for a fundraiser aimed to benefit the clinic. The photograph not only reinforces who will benefit, but shows that the proposal writers took the time to find or take the photograph. In the reader's mind, the writers' attention to this detail may reflect well on their ability to carry out the project—that is, the visual has an ethical appeal. Be sure to make clear what the image or photograph is through a label or other acknowledgment.

Production notes. For proposals to outside sponsors, consider using heavyweight paper and binding the proposal in a professional (not school) report cover or notebook. Pages should lie flat in the binding, so that the document does not suddenly close up during reading.

TIPS for proposals

- Make a good first impression with the design of the cover or title page.
- If you use any images, consider how they convey the overall community benefits of the project.
- Be sensitive to potential bias in choosing images.
- Provide a visually clear organization, using headings and other visual features of formal reports, such as callouts, captions, appendices, and the like. If the proposal is more than 2-3 pages, consider including an abstract and a table of contents.
- Let the readers interpret and compare information or options by including data graphics such as tables, charts, or line graphs.

Brochure

Purpose: Expressive and transactional, to publicize an organization or program
Rhetorical appeal: Ethos, logos
Copies: Many
Lifespan: Long—more than a year
Readers: Likely to be several targeted groups of readers who can benefit from the organization or program
Setting: Sitting or standing indoors. Readers may pick up the brochure from a display stand or at a meeting; or receive it in the mail.
Distractions and constraints: Setting may be noisy; nearby brochures in a display compete for attention; readers have seen many brochures and do evaluate their polish
Reading goals: Skimming and scanning, then searching. Reading is voluntary.
Order of reading: Cover panel, then one of the panels inside the fold, then browsing. Analyze sequence of information and visuals carefully.
Reader's immediate action: Comprehend the group's or program's mission and key activities, decide if it will benefit the reader, act to get more information
Format: Usually a six- or eight-panel folded sheet (6-panel: 8.5" x 11"; 8-panel: 8.5" x 14").
Visual flexibility: Considerable freedom within certain expected brochure conventions
Visual/text ratio: Cover panel primarily visual with key text; other panels balance text and visual elements

Visual features. To persuade readers to pick up the brochure and form a clear, favorable impression of the organization or program, attractive design, images, and layout are key. The cover panel attracts readers to the brochure. Color and some boldness of design can help. To convey basic information without overwhelming, a brochure needs clear sequencing for the specialized format and ample white space (chunking of text blocks). Avoid crowding the panels with text. Contact information must be easy to pick out.

Production features. The number of copies needed and the long lifespan of brochures may justify professional printing. If you plan to mail the brochure, one panel may need to be in standard postal format. Check with your post office for requirements.

TIPS for brochures

- Take an existing brochure that you like, open it flat, and analyze its structure. In what order do you read it? Storyboard the panels.
- Storyboard your own brochure.

- If your brochure will be placed in a display stand, give it a clear title and visual impact in the top half of the cover panel. A brochure for handing out and mailing may treat the cover panel more freely.

- Do not crowd the panels with text. Use ample white space, and put at least one visual on the inside panels.

- Apply borders and boxes with care and consistency in this "boxy" genre. White space often can do the job just as well as a box.

- Place contact information prominently.

- Get reader input.

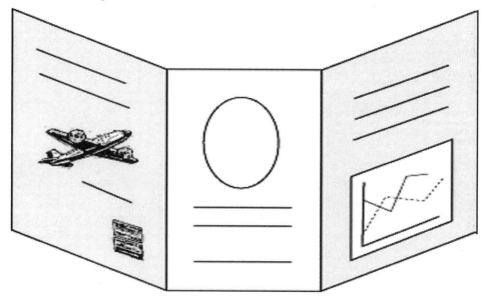

Figure 4.6 A sample brochure

Newsletter

Purpose: Transactional, to inform members of a group (such as a class, an organization, or a company) of newsworthy events; and expressive, to maintain group relationships and identity
Rhetorical appeal: Logos, ethos, and pathos
Copies: Many
Lifespan: Medium to long, depending on how often issued—weekly, monthly, quarterly, or annually

Readers: Primarily members of a group, but also outsiders who sponsor the group or who are prospective members

Setting: Sitting indoors

Distractions and constraints: The reading setting may be public (as a lobby or waiting room) and noisy. At work or home, other tasks compete for attention—the newsletter will likely be of low priority to many readers. Moreover, as with brochures, readers have seen many newsletters.

Reading goals: Skimming and scanning, then searching. For some articles, reading to comprehend the whole. Reading is voluntary and may depend on how much the reader identifies with the group. Relatively few readers will read the entire newsletter.

Order of reading: Browsing, sometimes sequential

Reader's immediate action: Reaffirm favorable impression of group; locate and comprehend items of importance to herself or himself; for one or two items, may note upcoming events or take action such as contacting another person

Format: Typically one, two, or four full-size sheets (8.5 x 11"), stapled; or printed on 11x17 sheets and folded

Visual flexibility: Considerable freedom

Visual/text ratio: Text and visual elements balance

Visual features. Newsletters are organized for print browsing, to attract readers through a pleasing, coherent design to a variety of types of information and articles. Like brochure design, newsletter design is a subspecies to itself, with many elements to consider. Visuals and white space are important to balance text. The short paragraphs in journalistic style are themselves a visual feature. Clip art has more uses in newsletters than in perhaps any other genre. The design should be tested with group members but also sponsoring readers.

Production notes. Newsletters that have a long lifespan—six months or a year—and are intended to represent the group to outsiders (as for funding or support or recruiting) may well be printed professionally.

TIPS for newsletters

*   Take an existing newsletter that you like, and analyze its structure. In what order do you read it? How do your eyes move over the pages? What do you focus on first? Look at the pages, columns, and visuals. Storyboard the pages.
*   Storyboard your own newsletter.
*   Take advantage of readers' tendency to view the page from top left to bottom right in a slanted "Z" pattern.

- Try a grid (see Chapter 5) to maintain an overall consistency among the pages without sacrificing interest and visual flexibility.

- Try using white space to group and frame areas. Use boxes and borders sparingly.

- Stick to two fonts—at most three—and use them consistently.

- Keep in mind that newsletter reading is voluntary and often serves as much to maintain a group's identity as to give factual information. Interesting visuals, such as photographs of members and participants, help maintain that identity and keep readers involved.

- In choosing clip art or images, be sensitive to readers' backgrounds, including gender, race, and class.

- Refine the design with reader input.

A Quarterly Outlook from School Faculty

SPRING 1999

Big Time Article

By Joseph Hooper

Time after Time the clock ticks on. Too bad I cannot stop it nor speed it up. I would slow time down when I am sleeping and speed it when I am working. I guess if I had that much control on time, there would be no need for time, and life would boring. What? Time keeps us sharp and functional. Without time everything would happen at once. Imagine what kind of mess that would be. It would be total chaos. Time after Time the clock ticks on. Too bad I cannot stop it nor speed it up. I would slow time down when I am sleeping and speed it when I am working. I guess if I had that much control on time, there would be no need for time, and life would boring. What? Time keeps us sharp and functional. Without time everything would happen at once. Imagine what kind of mess that would be. It would be total chaos.

Time after Time the clock ticks on. Too bad I cannot stop it nor speed it up. I would slow time down when I am sleeping and speed it when I am working. I guess if I had that much control on time, there would be no need for time, and life would boring. What? Time keeps us sharp and functional. Without time everything would happen at once. Imagine what kind of mess that would be. It would be total chaos. Time after Time the clock ticks on. Too bad I cannot stop it nor speed it up. I would slow time down when I am sleeping and speed it when I am working. I guess if I had that much control on time, there would be no need for time, and life would boring. What? Time keeps us sharp and functional. Without time everything would happen at once. Imagine what kind of mess that would be. It would be total chaos.

nor speed it up. I would slow time down when I am sleeping and speed it when I am working. I guess if I had that much control on time, there would be no need for time, and life would boring. What? Time keeps us sharp and functional. Without time everything would happen at once. Imagine what kind of mess that would be. It would be total chaos.

Time after Time the clock ticks on. Too bad I cannot stop it nor speed it up. I would slow time when I am sleeping and speed it when I am working. I guess if I had that much control on time, there would be no need for time, and life would boring. What? Time keeps us sharp and functional. Without time everything would happen at once. Imagine what kind of mess that would be. It would be total chaos. Time after Time the clock ticks on. Too bad I cannot stop it nor speed it up. I would slow time when I am sleeping and speed it when I am working. I guess if I had that much control on time, there would be no need for time, and life would boring. What? Time keeps us sharp and functional. Without time everything would happen at once. Imagine what kind of mess that would be. It would be total chaos.

IN NEXT QUARTERS ISSUE...

How to feed your kid?
How to see your kid?
How to stop your kid from crying?
How to comb your kids hair?

Figure 4.7 Newsletter by Joseph D. Hooper

Presentation slides

Purpose: Transactional, to support an informative or explanatory speech and to convey the ethos of the speaker and the speaker's organization

Rhetorical appeal: Logos, ethos, and in some cases pathos

Copies: One, but slides or files can be copied

Lifespan: Varies from brief to long

Readers: Meeting participants who already have an interest in the general subject area

Setting: Sitting indoors, often in darkened room

Distractions and special constraints: Reading is not voluntary. Readers cannot control the pace, focus, or viewing angle of slides, nor can they review previous slides. The setting may have poor screen lighting; the room may not be darkened enough to see well; there may be distracting noise from latecomers or in adjoining hallways. Business people may be tired of the special effects of some presentation software.

Reading goals: Skimming and scanning, then searching; some evaluation

Order of reading: Sequential (controlled by speaker)

Reader's immediate action: Take notes; ask for clarification or expansion

Format: slides, transparencies, or a computer generated sequence projected onto a screen. Typical orientation is wide (landscape) rather than long (portrait).

Visual flexibility: Some freedom, but constraints by topic and field expectations of this genre

Visual/text ratio: Text and visual elements balance, the visual including ample blank or "white" space.

Visual features. Most speeches and short talks need visuals. Transparencies or computer-generated slides projected onto a screen are standard. The keys to good slides are 1) visual support of the speech and 2) a presentation format that everyone can see and read. Because reading is not voluntary and viewers cannot control the sequence or pace, your first duty is not to irritate this captive audience with unreadable, dull, annoying, offensive, or overly cute visuals. For support of the speech, the slides should not reproduce the speaker's notes word for word but orient the audience, keep them interested, and visually clarify complex information. The presentation format of slides is also critical, especially the size of the type and images. The clear viewing area for overhead projection is smaller than the lighted area, limiting the amount of material that any one panel can hold.

TIPS for presentation slides

General:

- To orient the audience, use a title slide followed by an overview of the main points, then a series of well-organized main points with subpoints—like an outline.

- Use key phrases or short sentences, preferably in parallel grammatical structure, rather than long sentences.

- Apply highlighting and indenting consistently.

- Make the color scheme, format of visuals, and fonts consistent from slide to slide.

- Keep ample margins on all four sides.

- Remember that it takes up to two minutes to discuss a slide.

- Try your slides beforehand with the same type of equipment and room that you will have for your speech.

Visual elements:

- Use large, simple tables and graphs to clarify complex information. Label these clearly.

- In your talk, make clear the point of each table and graph.

- Use clip art, scanned photographs, or other images for variety and interest, but keep these simple. Test images for cultural, racial, and gender bias.

Type:

- For small classrooms and small meeting rooms with ordinary projection equipment, use type that is 16 points or larger. Presentation software such as Microsoft PowerPoint® typically employs 44-point type for headings and 32-point type for main text items. Remember that middle-aged or older viewers (such as many college faculty and business people) often cannot read the smaller type.

- Do not crowd text onto a slide. Instead make another slide.

- Use no more than two fonts in your presentation. Choose well-known, legible fonts that contrast with each other, such as Arial and Times.

Color and special effects:

- Choose colors for images, text, and background that have good figure-ground contrast. Place dark on light and light on dark. For example, place dark blue text on a white or light yellow background rather than light blue text on a yellow background.

- Avoid highly patterned backgrounds that make text less legible.

- If you are presenting from a computer, you may wish to control the flow of information and keep your audience's interest with animated effects to bring in text. Keep the effects simple and reasonably consistent. Do not repeat them to the point of annoying viewers.

Web site

Purpose: Varies greatly. For example, an organizational site may promote the organization and its mission or issues (transactional, expressive, and artistic); maintain its identity among its members (expressive); and give pertinent information to members and outsiders, especially links to other resources (transactional). Analyze your purpose and audience carefully before designing.

Rhetorical appeal: Logos, ethos, and pathos

Copies: Many, each produced on the individual reader's browser

Lifespan: Can vary from days to more than a year, depending on purpose

Readers: In theory, the entire Internet; in practical terms, a small group or set of groups

Setting: Indoors sitting at a networked computer, though personal digital assistants, cellular phones, and other wireless devices are changing this

Distractions and special constraints: All the constraints of screen reading and Web browsing

Reading goals: Skimming, scanning, and searching. Readers move from keyword to key-word or link to link rather than sequentially. They rarely read to comprehend the whole. Reading is voluntary and may depend on 1) how much the reader identifies with the group or issue or 2) how the site compares in content and attractiveness with other sites. There is tremendous competition from other sites.

Order of reading: Link to link or browsing—rarely sequential

Reader's immediate action: Gain a sense of site's mission and main information; decide if the site is worthwhile in content or of benefit to reader; link to more information or other sites; bookmark the site for reading again; act to get more information.

Format: One or more linked Web "pages" of any length, viewed on screen

Visual flexibility: Considerable freedom

Visual/text ratio: Visual elements predominate over text

Visual features. In this new medium, the rules are constantly being rewritten. Web sites need visual impact, good organization, clear navigation, and a sense of interactivity. Consistency of visual organization can help keep readers oriented among the pages of the site. In addition to the following tips, see the section on storyboarding (later in this chapter), as well as the principles of page and screen layout (Chapter 5) and the sample makeovers (Chapter 7).

TIPS for Web sites

General:

- Take an existing Web site that you like and analyze its structure. In what order do you read it? Look at the design and storyboard the screens.
- Storyboard your own Web site, showing how pages are linked.
- Take advantage of readers' tendency to scan for links by giving them links on each page.
- Maintain a consistent look across the pages of your site so readers know they are still in it.
- Try a grid (see Chapter 5) to create consistency without sacrificing interest and visual flexibility.
- Create consistent and usable navigation controls.
- Test your site on different computers and browsers, as well as with your intended readers.

Type:

- Use short paragraphs and about 20-40 characters (up to eight words) per line.
- Break up very long pages, which require readers to keep scrolling, into several shorter pages.
- Avoid italic text, which is hard to read on screen.
- For legibility, put dark text on a light background and light text on a dark background.

Color, visuals, and effects:

- Avoid animations to no purpose. Also avoid annoying features such as "blink" tags.
- Avoid patterned backgrounds behind text. They reduce legibility.
- Apply color not only for interest but also to maintain site identity.
- Use a "browser-safe" palette to help control the variation of different browser settings.
- Reduce the size of images for faster loading, so that readers don't leave the site in frustration.

Portfolio

Purpose: Demonstrate the breadth and depth of your writing to an instructor or potential employer

Rhetorical appeal: Ethos, logos, and pathos

Copies: Print—unique; Web or CD-ROM—multiple

Lifespan: Medium to long—a month to more than a year

Readers: Instructor, potential employers

Setting: Sitting indoors, possibly at a networked computer, normal reading distance

Distractions and constraints: Time pressure; may need to read with the writer present, as at an interview; may need instructions for accessing Web or electronic portfolio. Some readers will be very familiar with portfolios and others will have little or no experience.

Reading goals: Scanning, searching, and evaluating. Some competition from other portfolios.

Order of reading: Browsing (random access) or sequential

Reader's immediate action: Understanding of individual's special strengths and key skills in action; evaluation against other students or candidates or the standards of the job

Format: Bound print pages; linked Web pages; CD-ROM

Visual flexibility: Considerable freedom

Visual/text ratio: Text predominates with visual accents and organizers

Visual features. A portfolio is a unique genre, with much opportunity for visual creativity, yet it calls for many of the navigational features of more conventional long documents. Because it projects your ethos and because readers may be rushed or unfamiliar with portfolio layouts, the portfolio should have a unified look, visual impact that supports your ethos and the communicative purpose, and clear organization. A repeated visual element, such as a colored border, or a visual metaphor or theme, can help unify the different types of writing that portfolios usually have. Likewise, features such as a contents page and overviews of individual sections' help to orient readers, letting them know the context for particular documents and pointing them to special features. There is a place for personal expression here, as long as you take your audience's age and reasons for reading into account. Instructors and fellow students are likely to be interested in personal expression that implies your individual growth. Employers are less interested in expression than in clear structure and easy access that demonstrates your potential organizational skills on the job. (Instructors who are reading a stack of portfolios appreciate good organization, too.) Screen-based portfolios should follow the guidelines for screen layout and navigation.

Production features. The importance of portfolios justifies spending time to create a consistent "interface" with title, contents, and overview information linked visually by typeface and layout—and color or images, if you choose those. If time and resources permit, printing the different documents in a consistent way can also unify a portfolio. However, portfolio readers also expect and enjoy the variety of documents that they encounter, as long as the individual pieces are easy to access. Binding print documents in a folder or cover helps the reader handle them. Oversized documents (larger than 8.5" x 11") can be placed in folder pockets.

TIPS for portfolios

- For a simple but effective portfolio, create a cover page, a contents page, and section separators. Unify these with a simple visual theme.
- Repeat a visual feature—a border, an image—to unify the parts of the portfolio.
- Or slightly vary a visual feature—for example, by changing a color, or by adding a new visual element to each section—to show a progression or tell a visual story.
- Try to use a folder or binder that lets the pages lie flat.
- Avoid using a large envelope to hold your portfolio. It is harder to open than a folder or binder, and discourages the reader from browsing pages.
- Also avoid putting multiple-page documents in clear plastic sleeves if you expect the reader to look at each page.
- Test your electronic portfolio to ensure that it can be accessed by the reader's type of computer and software.

Thumbnails and storyboards

Two tools from the world of graphic design and film are very helpful to writers planning visual design. A **thumbnail** is a small, quick, rough sketch—like a doodle. Thumbnails are easy to draw, yet they give the essence of a visual idea to build on. You can sketch thumbnails of individual pages/screens, an intended illustration, image, chart, photograph, detail of typography, or layout feature. Label the drawings and their features so you'll recall what they mean. If you are working alone, thumbnails let you see your ideas and set the stage for more polished versions. If you are collaborating with others, thumbnails are an excellent brainstorming and conferencing tool.

A **storyboard** is a sequence of thumbnails, with commentary. Storyboards are used extensively in filmmaking, and more recently in multimedia development. In our terms, they are most useful for multi-panel genres that unfold to the reader through time. Beside each sketch, you record what is happening and how the reader navigates to the next panel. If your project is complex, it helps to enlarge the sketches and to put each one on a separate sheet of paper, so that they can be rearranged. The classic collaborative storyboard is posted on a wall so that all involved can study it, make suggestions, and rearrange the parts.

For a large Web site with many visuals and intricate navigation, consider a kind of super-storyboard. Multimedia designer and author Lisa Lopuck has noted that page or screen design is static, whereas multimedia is dynamic. She suggests imagining your site as "a series of environments, or 'places,'" such as a house (9), or a park, library, busy intersection—you get the picture. Each room or place within the house serves a purpose and supports distinctive activities. Jot down the places in this metaphoric environment, and begin assigning activities to those places. Make a schematic drawing of the relationships of these places and activities. Then create a storyboard for each place, finally bringing them together via the larger metaphor of house, park, and so on.

Figure 4.9 shows the thumbnail sketches and initial storyboard that Michelle Slater used to begin designing the home page (index.htm) for the Greenville Church of Christ. The top portion is a thumbnail sketch for the screen that allowed Michelle to decide where different kinds of information would be located, such as placing the "Who," "Where," "What," "See," and "Link" navigation links in a frame on the left side of the screen. The thumbnail also allowed Michelle to describe the "story" of what will happen when the users interact with the page in specific ways. For example, when the users "rollover" the image of a globe in the frame on the right hand side of the screen, the image will change to the Greenville Church of Christ logo. Or when users rollover the "Who" link, the graphic expands from the single word "Who" to the more descriptive "Who We Are." Michelle also used the thumbnail at the top to make decisions about color and background choices, such as the use of "dark gray text" for the right hand frame and the "ghosted image of collaged faces" as the background.

On the bottom third of her storyboard, Michelle also worked out the storyboard for what pages users would see when they clicked on the "Who," "Where," or other links. With this heirarchically arranged "map" for her site, Michelle knew all the names of the pages she needed for her site, making the site much easier for her first to create and then later to update and maintain.

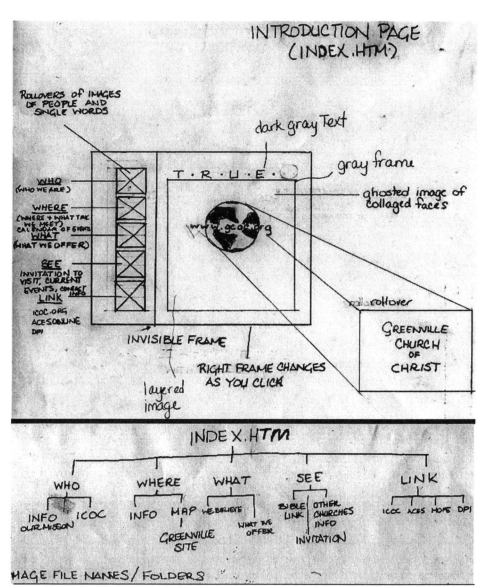

Figure 4.8 Storyboard for Web pages by Michelle Slater

Planning worksheets

The following worksheets can help you plan what visuals to include, where to place them in your document, and how to produce them. In rhetoric, these planning tools are sometimes called "heuristics." You should adapt these to your purposes. There is no wrong way to do them. As you fill in the analysis worksheet, refer to the sections analyzing various genres in this chapter. That may help you complete the worksheet. Also be sure to think carefully about your particular document, your readers, and its significance, as well as your facilities and time constraints. You may need many more thumbnails and storyboards than are provided in the second worksheet, plus more task analyses than are given in the third worksheet.

> **NOTE:** Check with your instructor for specific requirements about the format of visuals and the means for producing them. For example, your document may have specific guidelines for incorporating visual information, or you may be required to use certain charting or presentation software.

Summary

- Plan the visuals for your document as carefully as you plan the writing.
- As you develop visuals, consider your purpose, readers, and resources—people, time, money, and equipment.
- Plan for input from potential readers before you produce the final visuals.
- Use thumbnails and storyboards as planning tools.

Notes

[1]We thank Dr. Barbara Heifferon and her advanced technical writing students, fall 1998, for this example.

Visual Planning 1—Rhetorical Analysis

Project title
Genre

Purpose

relationship with readers
visual flexibility
lifespan
format
publication method and copies
significance

Readers

number—plus names of specific readers
age, range of ages
education, job
gender, race, class, culture
familiarity with similar documents
setting for reading
goals for reading
skim, scan, search, read receptively, read critically

Resources

production people
names, skills, availability
specific viewers (to give feedback)
names, availability
facilities
hardware, software, materials, supplies
time—deadlines
costs

What visual ideas do these genre, purpose, reader, and resource issues give you?

What visuals do you think you should avoid?

Visual Planning 2—Storyboarding

Project title

Genre (multi-panel)

Describe what is happening in this panel.

thumbnail of panel 1

Describe what is happening in this panel.

thumbnail of panel 2

Describe what is happening in this panel.

thumbnail of panel 3

Visual Planning 3—Tasks and Timeline

Project title

Put key items from worksheets 1 and 2 here as tasks, such as "find a picture of __,"
"make a chart to show ___," "get photo developed," "edit clip art," "practice presentation
with slides." Then connect tasks to the time line.

Time line

project start   **project end**

TASK   TASK
People   People
Resources   Resources
Estimated time to complete   Estimated time to complete

TASK   TASK
People   People
Resources   Resources
Estimated time to complete   Estimated time to complete

TASK   TASK
People   People
Resources   Resources
Estimated time to complete   Estimated time to complete

Visual Planning 4—Reader Input

Reader's name

Date   **Location**

What is your impression of this document?

Would you pick it up to read it? Why, or why not?

What do you think of the overall look of the document?

What do you think of the visuals in it—pictures, illustrations, tables, charts?

Comment on what you see as the point of each visual.

What is your impression of the authors or designers of this document? Can you point to places in the document that make you feel that way?

What suggestions do you have for visuals?

CHAPTER 5

Creating Pages and Screens

The basic design element of print documents is the page; that of electronic documents is the screen. The concepts of Gestalt psychology and genre provide starting points for the layout of pages and screens.

The following guidelines are strategies, not recipes. Work with one or two principles at a time to gain a feel for the visual elements. Do several versions of a page or screen and compare them, using these concepts as analytic tools.

> **NOTE:** These guidelines apply best to genres that have some visual flexibility, such as settings for poems and graffiti, flyers, fact sheets, brochures, newsletters, Web sites, and portfolios. They are less useful for genres that specify exact formatting rules, such as academic papers. See Chapter 2 for a discussion of rigid and flexible genres.

Gestalt-based principles

If you can create effective 1) figure-ground contrast and 2) visual groupings through proximity and similarity, you will have learned the most important perceptual principles of layout. The following principles are based mainly on Gestalt principles, with additions from semiotic theory, human factors research, and modernist theories of design. These ideas will add subtlety of organization to your documents.

Treat the page or screen as a background space

Readers approach documents as composed of text and visuals "on" a background, the visual field or Gestalt of the page or screen. Take advantage of this perceptual tendency.

As you place text and visuals, do a *squint test*: hold documents at arm's length or stand away from the screen and squint to become aware of the major areas of the field. Look at the relationships of the parts to each other and to the whole visual field. Make thumbnails (small sketches of the pages or screens) to stay aware of the overall Gestalt.

Use white space to advantage

- White space, or blank background space, defines what is placed "on" the page or screen.
- Use white space to group and separate.
- Use lack of contrast for continuity of text.
- Chunk text for scanning and searching genres.
- Be careful of extra space that wrongly groups your information.
- Examine the shapes that the white space creates. The visual field is created as much by these shapes as by the figures on it.
- Screens require even more blank space, up to 40 to 60 percent of the visual field (Coe 221).

Put dark text on a light background, or light text on a dark background

To stand out from the background, text must contrast in *value* from that background. *Value* is a graphics term meaning the relative lightness or darkness of a color. The lightest is white; the darkest is black. Use very dark text on light backgrounds. Alternatively, use light text on very dark backgrounds.

Black text on a white background is the most legible. The reverse, white or light text on a black background, has good contrast, but may be considered less legible because it is less common. Only put light on dark for short stretches of text—and sparingly.

On screens, where you usually have color available, be careful to choose colors that contrast in value. For example, don't put bright red text on a bright royal blue background. If those colors were reduced to black and white, they would be one shade of gray on another shade of gray—hard to read.

> **TIP:** One way to check the values of screen text and background colors is to take a screen capture of your text. Then open the image in an image-editing program such as Adobe Photoshop™. Temporarily change the mode to "grayscale" to see if the text stands out against the background.

Some background choices are more a matter of acculturation and preference than perception. Bright, pure colors like yellow may provide good figure-ground contrast for dark text.

However, because yellow is unusual for backgrounds, it may not be a good choice for extended reading on screens.

Avoid patterned screen backgrounds that reduce the legibility of text

Patterned backgrounds can substantially reduce the figure-ground contrast of text. That is particularly true on screens, where the resolution (fineness of detail) is considerably less than we expect from the printed page. Text superimposed on highly patterned backgrounds may be almost illegible. Many of the backgrounds available for Web sites and computer slide presentations fail this test.

Create a focal point on the page or screen

Readers focus first on the dominant visual, whether that is a picture or a contrasting area of type.

◆ Use images—photographs, well-chosen clip art, to focus attention on the covers of newsletters, brochures, and other genres that readers pick up voluntarily.

◆ On an unbroken page of text, as in the middle of a brochure or newsletter, use a *pull quote* or other simple visual feature to create a focal point.

**A pull quote is a quote
"pulled" from an article
for visual emphasis.**

Figure 5.1 Pull quote

Make contrasts easy to discern—bold and simple

As readers cope with the complex structure of a page or screen, they look for visually-distinct items. When you add new typefaces or other elements, make sure that they are clearly different in size and structure from others in the field.

If necessary, use highlighting—such as ***drop shadows***—to increase figure-ground contrast. Be careful, however, to keep such highlighting simple.

On computer screens, small, delicate graphic or type features may not be visible. Design screens with heavier, coarser elements that can withstand this degradation.

Consider the global as well as local effects of contrast. The reader may be overwhelmed by many unrelated contrasts.

Plan for color

Consider your document's audience and apply the principles of contrast, grouping, and similarity as you plan for color. See Chapter 2 for additional guidelines. On pages, remember that color may add life and interest, but also expense. On both pages and screens, limit colors to six. That includes the color of background, text, and (on Web pages) links (Coe 223).

Place elements close to each other to create visual associations

One of the most effective changes you can make to your documents is to apply the principle of proximity. The human eye discriminates among small changes in spacing and tends to group items that are visually close.

- Place headings close to the text they introduce.
- Make sections visually distinct. Use white space as the primary separator.
- Place figures and illustrations close to the text that interprets them.
- Create associations by juxtaposing items.

> **TIP:** Instead of creating headings yourself, use a heading "style" in your word processor. These styles often adjust the standard vertical spacing by placing the heading further from preceding text and closer to its associated text. Or, without using a style, you may also bypass the standard single and double-spacing format options. Reduce the space between a heading and its text by several "points." Add several points of spacing before the heading. That way you create a "frame" of space around the heading and the associated text.

Show relationships visually

Recall the principle of similarity: We tend to group items by their proximity (closeness to each other), their position and orientation on the page, their shape, and their color or texture.

Repeat visual features to unify

Repeat an element more than once in the page, screen, document.

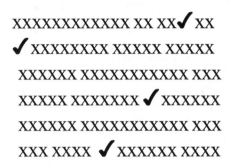

Figure 5.2

Readers will tend to group the repeated items because of their similarity of shape.

Keep alignments strong and simple

The eye follows the line created by text edges. That is the Gestalt principle of good continuation, therefore keep alignments strong and simple.

- In general, keep one major alignment in a document: left, center, right.
- Try not to mix alignments on a page or screen.
- Align each element with something else in the visual field.
- With screen documents (slides and Web pages), remember that the center of the screen will likely be in sharper focus, so avoid extreme left or right alignments on screen.

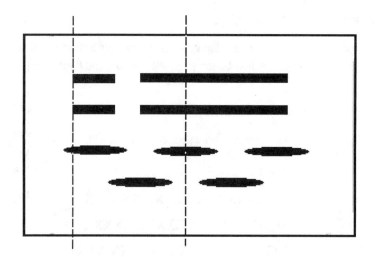

Figure 5.3 Mixed left and center alignment on a screen

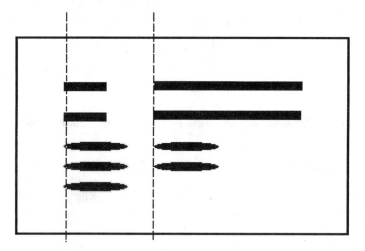

Figure 5.4 Consistent left alignment, each element lined up with another

Balance elements on the page or screen

Visual balance is more than symmetry. Rather, consider the analogy of balance in physics. Two people of different weight can balance on a seesaw if the lighter person sits farther from the fulcrum and the heavier person sits closer to it. Symmetry—like aligning along the center of the page—maintains balance because each half of the field is a mirror image of the other. (In our analogy, both people weigh the same.) Symmetrical layouts are very stable. Yet asymmetrical, balanced layouts create tension and therefore interest. If you think that your readers may not automatically read your document, you might try this type of layout.

- Balance a large picture or text block with one or more small but distinctive items placed **higher** and **farther** from the center of the page or screen.
- Try unequal visual areas to create tension and interest.
- Remember that balance is visual, not mechanical.

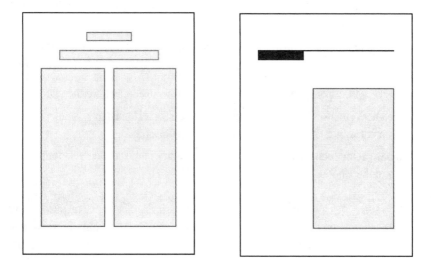

Figure 5.5 Balance: symmetry and asymmetry

The two page layouts in Figure 5.5 illustrate different approaches to balance. The two-column layout on the left is symmetrical, like a mirror image. The asymmetrical layout on the right uses the high contrast of the small, black rectangle in the header to balance the lower tonal density of the large, gray block.

Avoid unnecessary design elements

Hundreds of design elements are available for page layout. That does not mean you should use them all. For example, a box or border may seem to provide instant grouping or closure, but it is often unnecessary. Indeed, it may draw so much attention as to distract readers from the rest of the page or screen.

Decide if a design feature is needed

- Use the squint test to see the whole effect of your design.
- Decide what you want to emphasize most.
- Consider subtracting features one by one.
- Instead of eliminating a feature, try to:
  —make an item paler or smaller, so that it has less prominence on the page

  —change its color

  —give important items more size or contrast

  —replace a full box with a border on one side

  —use white space, shading, or a change in type size to achieve the effect.
- If the feature is markedly different from everything else, try to match its shade, color, shape, or alignment with another element to create a relationship.
- If you have many such features, go back to the squint test to see their relationships to each other and the whole.

When you do use a special design element, treat it rhetorically. The genre or purpose may call for additional interest on the page or screen. Whatever you choose should be visually simple, applied consistently, and in keeping with the overall visual design and purpose of the document.

Genre-based principles

As Chapter 2 shows, what we expect to see is very much related to what we have seen in the past. Visual conventions are everywhere. Your documents will be more effective if they let readers employ their past experience with visual emphasis, layers, scanning of text, navigation, and illustrations. They also identify the genre of the document, so they are prepared for the particular visual conventions of that genre. Although they are closely related to the ideas in the previous section, the following guidelines take genre knowledge into greater account than those above.

Provide visual emphasis

In Western cultures, emphasis goes to **larger** items and to items **higher** in the visual field. Smaller items and items further down the page or screen are deemed less important. Therefore:

- Make more important information larger, or give it more visual weight.
- Put more important information higher in the visual field.
- Realize that actual size and emphasis may conflict. For example, a realistic array of sports equipment that includes a golf ball and a basketball will emphasize the basketball.

Create visual layers

- Use visual cues to link elements on a single page or screen.
- Use visual cues to connect multiple page or screen documents.
- For longer documents, create several independent layers that viewers can scan as they flip pages or move from screen to screen.

Take advantage of typical reading patterns

Readers may enter a document by looking at the dominant visual. In addition, Western readers search for continuation cues at bottom center or right (Kristof and Satran 91).

- Place the most important text close to the dominant visual.
- In newsletters, put *jumplines* (such as "Continued on p. 3") at the bottom center or right of articles that continue onto another page.
- On Web pages, put "Forward" or "Next" links and buttons to the right of the visual field.

Pay attention to interactions of layout with illustrations

As we have seen, readers tend to focus on images before text and focus on more representational images before more abstract images. The orientation of human figures in photos and clip art also affects the layout. Consider these conventions as you design:

- Time moves to the right.
- Pages open to the right.

- Faces turned toward the center of the page/screen lead viewers back into the visual field.
- Faces turned away from the center lead viewers out of the page or screen.

Consider the tone or personality of layouts

For example, take alignments:

- Centering creates a formal, conservative tone recalling the title pages of old books. Wedding and other invitations are often centered.
- Left alignment is standard for body text in Western documents. Its tone tends to be neutral, objective, scientific.
- Right alignment is rare for body text (but common for columns of numbers). It can create an unusual, "edgy" setting for some expressive documents.

Study the format of particular genres

Newsletter conventions, for example, are based on years of readers' and editors' experience with periodicals, especially newspapers. The layout of newsletters has a whole vocabulary and body of received wisdom, so does the design of resumes. The guidelines in this chapter touch on just the most basic conventions. For more detailed information about a particular genre, see Chapter 4 and the bibliography.

Treat multi-panel genres with special care

As we saw in Chapter 4, single-panel genres are the documents that readers generally see "all at once" (poems, logos, resumes, flyers, posters) while multi-panel genres—newsletters, brochures, Web pages—unfold to through time as readers turn pages, open folded sections, or click on links. Multi-panel genres require close attention to visual organization and navigation through the document.

In multiple page and screen documents, consider how much the reader sees at once and how much the reader needs to retain from panel to panel. Use the following guidelines to help you get started, and collect and analyze examples of documents that you like.

Give an overview of multi-panel documents

◆ Create a table of contents or navigation bar.

◆ Add an "in this issue" block on the front page of newsletters, Web sites, fact sheets.

◆ Write a short executive summary or abstract for proposals and reports.

Give consistent continuation and navigation cues

◆ Use "jumplines" to connect newsletter articles that are continued on another page.

◆ Put an *icon*, short *rule* (line), or *dingbat* (small visual symbol) at the end of newsletter articles to signify closure.

◆ Place navigation buttons and links in the same positions from screen to screen so readers can find them easily.

On Web pages, give links on each panel or screenful of text

Readers read Web text differently from print information. They scan for links as much as they engage in continuous reading. One rule of thumb is to provide about four links (text or graphical) for every 25 lines—a full screen—of text (Coe 222).

Use the order of reading to design panels

For example, readers tend to look at the cover of a brochure, then open it to a second panel before seeing the inside three panels. That gives you a "second front page" to engage your readers, so design the first two panels of a brochure as a sequence.

Design for the entire view

Consider everything the reader sees at once—the whole visual field.

◆ Design the interior pages of newsletters as a whole: a two-page *spread.*

◆ Design the inner three panels of a brochure as a three-page spread.

Try a grid to unify multiple panels

A *grid* divides the page or screen into rectangular areas and serves as a template for page or screen layout. A grid's main purpose is to help you maintain consistency among the pages or panels of a multiple-view document. However, a grid can also help you vary the layout without straying too far from your chosen format.

♦   Sketch different arrangements of material on the grid to see the overall look.

♦   Remember that columns need not be even.

♦   Remember that size equals emphasis.

Figure 5.6 Two-column and three-column grids for newsletters

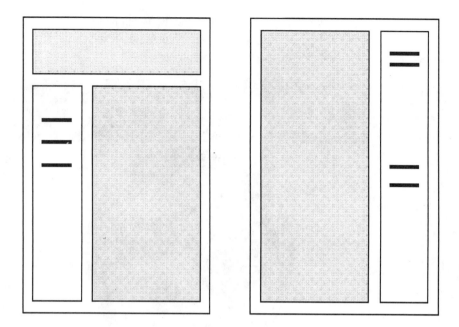

Figure 5.7 Flexible use of a three-column grid

Consider the differences between designing a "page" and designing a screen.

Because the Web is such a new medium, relative to printed media, it is easy for designers to forget that they really aren't designing a "page" *per se*. Indeed, what we routinely refer to as a "Web page" isn't really a "page" at all; it's just a convenient metaphor. However, like all metaphors, the analogy between a page and a screen breaks down and can become a trap for the unwary.

One of the principal differences between designing for the screen is that web designers have far less control over what the user actually sees. Whereas the author of a print document can depend that the size of a page will remain relatively stable, the web designer has little control over the size of users' computer monitors, the resolution of those monitors, whether or not the users have their browser software maximized, or even what fonts the users might be using or have installed on their systems.

Failing to keep these factors in mind lead to disastrous results, as can be seen in the example below. The designer of this Web page created it for a screen running at a resolution of 1024x768 pixels since that was the resolution he used on his computer.

Figure 5.8 Soccer page at 1024x768 resolution

Unfortunately, for another Web user running her monitor at a resolution of 640x480, the page looks entirely different and is far, far less effective. For her, the burning soccer ball is almost entirely missing, and the team name and logo in the top frame are severely cropped. As a result, there's very little about this page resolution that indicates the primary purpose of this site to this particular user. Unless she's willing to invest a fair amount of time and energy in the site, she may never figure out that this is a Web site for the Clemson Raptors soccer team.

Another and perhaps even more vexing problem with the design of this Web "page" is that it requires the user to scroll. At a resolution of 640x480, over half of the "table of contents" for the site doesn't appear on the screen, requiring that the user scroll down in the left frame just to see what navigation options she has available to her. However, usability testing research has consistently shown that, when Web users are browsing or "surfing" a site, they do **not** scroll down on a page 90% of the time (Nielson 112).

110

Figure 5.9 Soccer page at 640x480 resolution

These two factors—the recognition that users tend not to scroll and the instability of a Web page's display size—are perhaps the major influences on a screen's design. They have the effect of privileging certain areas of the screen over others. Because objects that are placed in the upper left quadrant of a screen are more likely to be visible to users without the need for scrolling, they are usually the most important information the designer wishes to convey to users. Web designers often describe this phenomenon using a "real estate" metaphor.

Just as real estate agents will say that "location, location, location" determines the value of a house, Web designers have learned that information they place on the lower-right-hand quadrant of a screen occupies the least valuable "screen real estate." Consequently, Web authors tend to place company logos or visuals that influence users' understanding of the purpose or "branding" of a site at the top of the screen. This helps create a context that will allow the user to interpret the site more effectively. Navigation information is also critical since users want to know how to move around a site. Hence, navigation information is often located along the left edge of the screen.

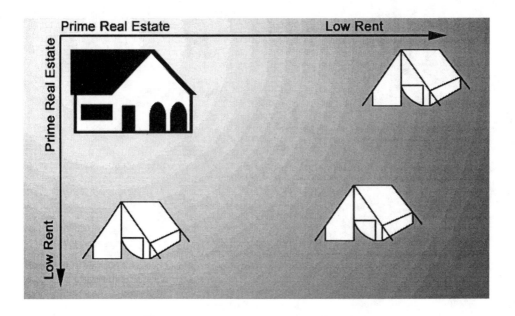

Figure 5.10 Screen real estate metaphor

As Web authors have come to understand the effect of screen real estate, they have increasingly abandoned designs based on the old "page" metaphor. New designs are emerging, and two of the most popular of these are known as the "inverted-L" and the "letterbox" format.

As its name implies, the inverted-L format looks like an "L" that has been turned upside down and flipped. The inverted-L is perhaps the most popular design found on the Web today, and there are a tremendous number of variations on it. For example, on very large, complex Web sites a designer might choose to reduce the size of the logo and name at the top in order to create space for a high-level navigation bar that will take users to major divisions in a site. Then the table of contents area along the left side might be used for navigation with the subsections of each major division.

Figure 5.11 Inverted-L format

Regardless of how the variation, however, the main point of the inverted-L is to maximize the impact of the available screen real estate.

The second popular type of design is known as the "letterbox" format. It is called "letterbox" because its elongated shape resembles the letterbox format used to show motion pictures on a television screen without cropping.

Figure 5.12 Web page in letterbox format

In the example here, the designer chose a letterbox design to avoid the screen real estate problems of having too much text on the screen. Typical of letterbox designs, this site uses a navigation bar or clickable graphic that may be viewed at resolutions of 640x480 and higher without cropping, distortion, or the need for scrolling. The navigation bar in this particular case is also a "rollover," so that, when the user places the cursor on top of a "clickable" area on the navigation bar, the graphic changes in order to signal some kind of navigation cues to the end user. Also, as is typical of letterbox designs, this site repeats the same design elements throughout the site. Users will find the same navigation bar using the same rollovers on every screen, and users will find the same header block with key words (in the same size and type of font) at the top of each screen, signaling the purpose and main idea of each screen to the users.

Consider the screen of Web pages as a complex visual field

Web design evolves quickly, but it is clear that Web readers expect a complex experience that is unlike print and even other online materials. The following advice on Web layout comes from Deb Staed, who teaches university faculty and students about Web and multimedia design. Deb uses the familiar "inverted-L" format.

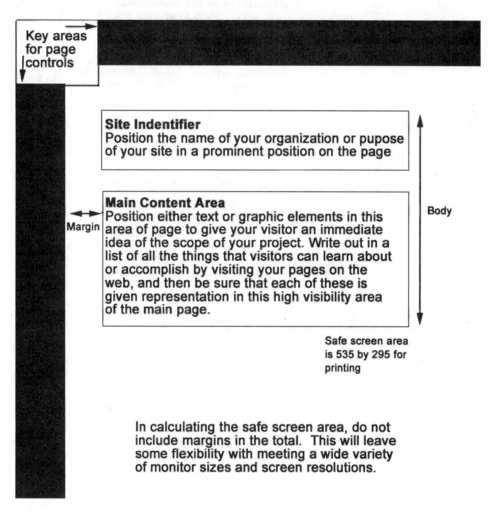

Figure 5.13 Whole Web page layout

115

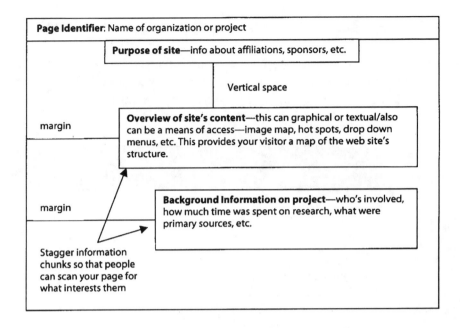

Page Identifier: Name of organization or project

Purpose of site—info about affiliations, sponsors, etc.

Vertical space

margin

Overview of site's content—this can graphical or textual/also can be a means of access—image map, hot spots, drop down menus, etc. This provides your visitor a map of the web site's structure.

margin

Background Information on project—who's involved, how much time was spent on research, what were primary sources, etc.

Stagger information chunks so that people can scan your page for what interests them

1) **Using margins** is important when presenting web text, especially if you expect your viewers to actually read online. For webtext, sanserif fonts, such as Verdanda, Univers, Myriad and Frutiger are generally more readable. Margins provide a stable line for your readers' eyes to return to when viewing a line of text. You can also use margins to call attention to certain content information.

2) **Use vertical white space** to indicate where one section ends and the other picks up; stay away from horizontal rules since they tend to trap sections of your page. Use vertical space to make distinctions between information types.

3) **Provide an overview of site's content.** (this includes possible actions that site supports as well as an indication of scope of information) For example if your site chronicles the life and times of Virginia Woolf, you would want to let folks know from your main page how comprehensive your coverage is.

Figure 5.14 Body section layout

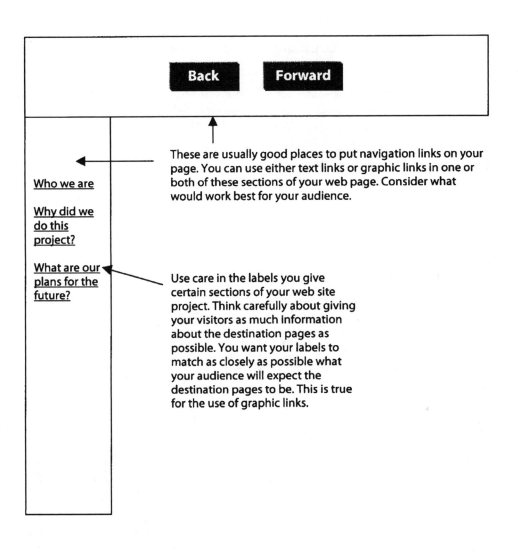

These are usually good places to put navigation links on your page. You can use either text links or graphic links in one or both of these sections of your web page. Consider what would work best for your audience.

Use care in the labels you give certain sections of your web site project. Think carefully about giving your visitors as much information about the destination pages as possible. You want your labels to match as closely as possible what your audience will expect the destination pages to be. This is true for the use of graphic links.

Figure 5.15 Navigation section layout

117

Consider a software template

Many word processing and desktop publishing programs provide models, or templates, of certain genres, such as resumes, brochures, newsletters, and Web pages. To use them, you simply choose a model from a file list. You are given a completed design that you then fill in with your own information. Using a template can not only save time, but also teach you about basic layout with less frustration than starting from scratch would. Templates do have problems. They are designed to showcase the software's features, many of which may be unsuited for your readers and purpose. They also are widely used by other people, so they are not especially original. See Chapter 4 for some common pitfalls regarding particular genres. When you use a template:

- Resist the urge to start typing immediately.
- Ask yourself if the design fits your document's purpose and readers.
- Plan where you will place your main text and visuals.
- Modify the layout, headings, and content for your purpose.
- Avoid "featuritis"—including features just because the template has them.
- Consider these guidelines.
- Get reader input.

Use familiar models to unify Web sites and portfolios

Web sites and portfolios tend to have parts or sections. These somewhat unusual genres also have less settled format conventions than other genres, and readers may not know what to expect. As a result visual design can be a way to unify the parts of the document.

For both Web sites and portfolios, it is common to treat the space as similar to a more familiar type of document or space. (As we saw in Chapter 4, Lisa Lopuck calls these "places.") That is, employing a metaphor or mental model can help readers correctly anticipate what will come and retain where they have been in the document. Common metaphors include books, maps, rooms, buildings, journeys, and stories. Make sure that the model is clear to readers.

If you become interested in layout, look for examples and advice from professional graphic designers in works like *The Non-Designer's Design Book* by Robin Williams and *The Makeover Book* by Roger C. Parker.

Summary

* Learn and try out one or two principles of layout at a time.

* Do multiple versions, and get reader input.

* Apply the Gestalt principles of figure-ground contrast and grouping.

* Be attentive to the many specialized layout features of particular genres.

Exercises

Collect several examples of print and on-screen documents that you like: brochures, fact sheets, flyers, newsletters, onscreen presentation slides, Web pages. For each:

1. Jot down what you like about the document.

2. "Squint" at it to blur the details and make the overall design elements stand out. Try sketching what you see—the main areas.

3. Then try to analyze your sketch—the layout—using some of the concepts in this chapter. Write your analysis on the sketch.

> **TIP for screen documents:** If the colors and flicker of the computer screen interfere with your analysis of a Web site or a presentation slide's layout, try this. Take a "screen capture" by pressing "Prnt Scrn" (on Windows-based machines). This copies the appearance of the screen to the Clipboard. Then open a paint program such as MICROSOFT PAINT™ and paste the image there. You can save and print the image in black and white to help you analyze it.

4. Instead of sketching the layout, try cutting out the basic shapes from colored construction paper and laying them on a background. Try moving the shapes around. This method is valuable because the coarser shapes encourage looking at the "big picture,"or Gestalt. For an elaboration of this technique, see Molly Bang, *Picture This: Perception and Composition* (Boston: Bulfinch-Little, Brown, 1991).

CHAPTER 6

Using Type

Type is the main visual feature of most documents. Learning to use type well can help organize your documents more clearly, make a better impression on readers, and let them read your documents more easily. This chapter considers two main issues:

1. how to choose legible type and

2. how to combine different typefaces.

To do that, we need a vocabulary for discussing type based on its structure and look.

By the way, *type* refers to all the alphabetic and numerical characters of documents, plus punctuation marks. A *typeface*, or *font*, is the design of a particular set of type. In this book, the terms typeface and font are used interchangeably.

How is type constructed?

All type has many visual features, starting with the look of individual letters.

Letterforms

Each capital and small letter has a form. Let's look closely at a few features of letterforms:

Figure 6.1 Graphics with serifs, x-height marked

121

Each letter in a typeface is made of strokes. Some typefaces, like this one, have small strokes on the ends of letters called *serifs*. The presence or absence of serifs is a way to distinguish among varieties of type. The height of small letters like *e*, *a*, *r*, and *n* is called the *x-height*. X-height is named for the space taken up by the letter *x*, and is a major factor in legibility.

In the following words, examine the differences in the shapes of letterforms, especially the ends of letters. (That is, are there serifs?)

1. graph   2. graph

3. **graph**   4. *graph*

Figure 6.2 Different shapes of letters

Samples 1, 2, and 4 have serifs while Sample 3 does not. The shape of the letter *g* also differs. The *x-height* of Sample 3 is also larger than the others, while Sample 1's letter *h* is taller than Sample 2's. Each of the four fonts creates a different tone. With its graceful curved lines and serifs, sample 1 has a traditional look, called *Old Style*. Sample 2 looks like a typewriter font; each letter takes up the same amount of space, and its serifs are typically flat, boxy slabs. Sample 3, with no serifs and large x-height, has a more contemporary look. It is a *sans serif* font. Sample 4 obviously imitates the look of handwriting and is called *script*.

Type is traditionally measured by height, in a printer's unit called a *point*. (There are approximately 72 points to the inch.) Yet different typefaces in the same size vary considerably in both their real and apparent height and width, so looking at the actual type on the page or screen is helpful. Notice the differences in size in these typefaces, all 18 points high:

Eighteen point   Arial

Eighteen point   Garamond Light Condensed

Eighteen point   Bookman Old Style

Eighteen point   **Impact**

Figure 6.3 Same point size, different apparent size

The impact of type is based on a combination of differences. In addition to size, letterforms also vary in thickness of strokes (called *weight*) and slant (called *direction*). Letters with both thick and thin strokes are said to have ***stress*** while letters with even strokes have no stress. The thick and thin strokes can be reminiscent of calligraphy. Contrast the effect of these features following pairs:

Big

small

Lightweight

Heavyweight

Vertical

Slanted

Stress

No stress

Figure 6.4 Contrasting type features

By its structure and weight, some type also seems best suited for titles and headings—*display type*. Decorative, unusual, and script fonts, as well as bold, heavy fonts of any structure, are in this category.

Newsletter
Newsletter

Figure 6.5 Display type

Fonts that can be read at length may be used in text passages as ***body type***, but they can also be used for display, in their larger sizes and heavier weights. This book, for example, is set in Garamond BookCondensed, a common font for body type.

Times New Roman

Fonts that can be read at length may be used in text passages as *body type*, but they can also be used for display.

Arial and Arial Black

Fonts that can be read at length may be used in text passages as *body type*, but they can also be used for display.

Figure 6.6 Body type

As you make choices for documents, try to notice the differences in type and begin using this basic vocabulary to discuss those differences.

What makes type more legible?

Both Gestalt and genre-based principles are important in increasing the legibility of text. By now you have heard the advice "Use enough figure-ground contrast" several times. Contrast between text and background is crucial for legibility, whether in display or body type. As explained in Chapters 1 and 2, several factors interact to affect reading behavior and thus legibility. These include the medium of the document (paper or screen), readers' genre knowledge, and their goals for reading. The classic study of legibility is by Miles A. Tinker. His results and those of other researchers have been summarized in technical and professional communication textbooks (Schriver, 274-75; Kostelnick and Roberts, 142-45; 190-92). The tips given in this chapter are based on Gestalt principles, legibility research, and accepted type conventions for Western genres.

Place type on a plain background that contrasts well in value

Black type on white background offers the best contrast for simple legibility. Reversed type—white or pale type on a black or dark background—is legible in headlines or short text elements. Use a heavier weight for reversed type.

For body text, use type of 10, 11, or 12 points

Smaller type is hard to read, especially for older readers.

For long passages, consider type with a large x-height

As we have seen, x-height is the height of small letters like *o* or *x*. A typeface with a fairly large x-height is usually more legible than type of the same size, but a smaller x-height.

Use ample leading

Besides type size and x-height, several other factors affect legibility. **Leading** (pronounced "ledding") is the vertical spacing between lines of type. Too little leading makes letters difficult to distinguish. Too much leading may interfere with the reader's forward progress through the text. Different typefaces may need somewhat different leading.

Too little leading makes letters difficult to distinguish. Too much leading may interfere with the reader's forward progress through the text. Different typefaces may need somewhat different leading.

Figure 6.7 Too little leading

Too little leading makes letters difficult to distinguish. Too

much leading may interfere with the reader's forward

progress through the text. Different typefaces may need

somewhat different leading.

Figure 6.8 Too much leading

As a rule, short passages—brochure copy, newsletter articles, text blocks in a resume—can take somewhat more generous leading than extended text (as reports or proposals) can. The latter requires enough leading to distinguish letters clearly, but not so much as to make lines drift away from each other during longer periods of reading.

> **TIP:** The standard leading—often called single spacing—for common word processing programs is typically the point size plus 2 to 2.5 points of extra space. The standard leading for 12-point type is therefore about 14 to 14.5 points. Up to 4 points of leading will give reasonable legibility. You can usually adjust the leading by using the line spacing format features of your software.

What about *double spacing*? That is a requirement for many academic papers, and you should follow the guidelines you are given. However, in print and online publications, double spacing is rare.

Adjust line lengths for legibility

As with leading, the length of lines affects legibility. In text passages, overly long and overly short lines both interfere with readers' ability to group words into meaningful units.

- For pages, make lines between 40 and 70 characters long.
- For screens, reduce the line length to 40-55 characters.

As with leading, the length of lines affects legibility. Overly long and overly short lines both interfere with readers' ability to group meaningful units. For pages, make lines between 40 and 70 characters long. For screens, reduce the line length to 40-55 characters.

Figure 6.9 Lines too long

As with leading, the length of lines affects legibility. Overly long and overly short lines both interfere with readers' ability to group meaningful units.

Figure 6.10 Lines too short

Consider type, leading, and line length together

Changing one of these factors affects the others. In the previous example, reducing the type size adds more characters per line—in effect increasing the line length. Make sure that your changes remain within the guidelines for legibility.

Watch for excess white space when you justify text

Short lines or narrow columns combined with *justified* text, as in the previous example, can create "rivers" of white space that wrongly group the information. (*Justification* or "full justification" aligns both the left and right edges of text passages by inserting small amount of extra space between words.) Even with longer lines, readers can be momentarily confused by this excess space.

Consider left-justified or "ragged right" alignments for body text

While fully justified text has a professional look, left-aligned text with a "ragged right" margin gets good marks for legibility. These results may have more to do with particular software or reader preferences than human factors. (For a review of research, see Schriver 269-71.) Left-justified text appears more informal. Consider alignment as part of your document's ethos.

Reduce the number of words broken by hyphenation

Too much hyphenation also interrupts the reader's grasp of words. Often excessive hyphenation is the result of shortening the lines, as in columns.

Too much hyphena-
tion also inter-
rupts the reader's grasp
of words. Often exces-
sive hyphenation is
the result of shor-
tening the lines,
as in col-
umns.

Figure 6.11 Too much hyphenation

127

Avoid setting multiple lines in capital letters

All capital letters create a "boxy" shape that seems to interfere with reading. This is especially true of *reversed type*, putting white or light letters on a dark background.

Avoid italics for lengthy passages; on screen, avoid italics completely

Italics are harder to read. On screen, the combination of thin, slanted lines and the *pixellation* (jagged, dot-like appearance) of letters is particularly hard to decipher.

Test your font choices with likely readers

Testing is especially important for Web pages, where different browsers interpret the colors and fonts differently. Remember, if a user doesn't have a font installed on his or her hard drive, you Web page design will be corrupted.

How can you use type effectively?

Clear organization and legibility are important, but so are the reader's interest and the ethos that you project. Type is a major element in your document's personality.

The array of fonts on word-processing and desktop publishing programs is both a pleasure and a challenge. A good beginning rule for combining fonts:

Stick to two or at most three fonts in any one document

Choose one font for body type and one for display—article titles, headings, pull-quotes. If you use a third, it may be a particularly striking font for the document's masthead or main title or other effect. However, remember that it helps to repeat any visual feature somewhere in the document. You may combine two display fonts in a variety of ways.

Use type consistently to help the reader organize and scan

Headings, pull-quotes, jump lines, and other text features that readers use as scanning layers should be consistent at each level.

Make bold distinctions between fonts

Combine typefaces that have definite contrasts in structure, weight, slant, or size. Better still, make sure that the fonts contrast in at least two ways. High contrast gets noticed by readers. Changes in weight—light vs. bold or extra bold—may be more noticed than actual changes of font (Schriver 274).

Avoid small changes in type size

The difference between 10-point type and 12-point type is not very noticeable. If you are sticking with a single font, make clear the size and weight differences of headings.

Remember that sans serifs often combine well with serif typefaces

It is a well-worn but safe guideline: Use sans serif fonts like Arial or Helvetica for headings and display type. Use an Old Style serif font like Times Roman, Palatino, Garamond or Goudy Old Style for body type. These contrast in structure. The built-in styles for body text and headings of many word processing programs incorporate this basic concept. The more traditional the audience or rigid the genre, the more likely that this combination will serve well.

Combine typefaces that reflect the ethos and tone of your document

Display type is a good way to express how you want readers to respond to your document.

Lively Newsletter for Schoolchildren
Flyer for a Lecture
Invitation to a Graduation
Proposal Cover

Figure 6.12 Samples of display type

Realize the limits of Web fonts

On the Web, where choices of fonts are limited because of the standards for Hypertext Markup Language (HTML), consider making the titles and headings into graphics rather than using the heading choices of HTML. You will be able to create more variety. If you do use HTML, try to limit yourself to Arial, Courier New, and Times New Roman.

If the rhetorical situation allows, use but don't abuse special type effects

There are hundreds of special type effects, such as *drop caps*, *letterspacing*, *drop shadows,* and text that is rotated or given a three-dimensional effect. Any one of these can create a focal point on your page or screen and help lead the reader into your document. In general, stick to one effect, used sparingly and consistently.

Drop caps lead readers into an article, focusing attention and drawing the eye down the page. Drop caps create a dramatic, formal effect. They hark back to medieval manuscripts and fine printed books.

LETTERSPACING

Putting small amounts of space between letters— letterspacing— can be an imposing treatment for mastheads, titles, and other emphatic display type.

Figure 6.13 Drop caps and letterspacing

Drop Shadows

are popular on the Web and in informal newsletters and brochures.

Figure 6.14 Drop shadows

Summary

- Type is the single most important element for readers, so it pays to learn to use it effectively.
- Noticing the structure of typefaces or fonts aids in using type well.
- There are two main uses of type:
    - —display type for titles, headings, and other distinctive features
    - —body type for text passages
- For legibility, make sure that the type contrasts clearly with the background.
- Avoid emphasis that obscures letterforms, such as multiple lines of all caps or italics.
- For greatest legibility of body type, choose a font with a large x-height.
- Stick to two or, at the very most, three fonts in a document.
- When you combine fonts, remember the principles of contrast and similarity:
    - —make the contrasts between the fonts bold
    - —create consistent visual relationships in your use of each font

Exercises

1. Describe each of the following fonts. Are its features:

- Lightweight or heavyweight?
- Slanted or upright?
- Script (like hand lettering) or detached?
- Decorative or plain?

131

- With serifs or without?
- Stressed (having both thick and thin strokes in a letter) or without stress (having even strokes)?
- What tone does the font project? Who would use it, and for what?
- Would you say that the font is for display type or body type, or both?

Layout, fonts, graphics

Layout, fonts, graphics

Layout, fonts, graphics

Layout, fonts, graphics

Layout, fonts, graphics

2. Examine the large printed letters on one or more of the following:

- a book cover
- an ad
- the package of a common food or household item
- a sign for a business, campus, or other building

Analyze the features of the typeface or faces. What message do they convey?

3. Take a favorite quotation, poem, or scrap of graffiti. Select a font that expresses the words, and create a simple visual setting for the lines. Add a second font if you like. Experiment with line lengths and spacing, even special effects. Try two or three versions, and ask other readers to tell you what they experience when they look at the different versions.

CHAPTER 7

Adding Images and Information Graphics

Much visual information is embedded in choices of type and overall layout. Yet for many documents you will want to add images (photographs, drawings, clip art) or information graphics (tables, charts, graphs, maps). This chapter contains tips for using images and information graphics effectively. Some of these apply Gestalt principles:

- framing a graphic with white space to achieve figure-ground contrast
- placing a graphic close to its related text to take advantage of proximity
- making two variables on a graph distinctive in shape or color to using a line drawing rather than a photograph to help viewers distinguish the structure

Other tips rely on research findings, such as being aware of the minimum size for colored items. Still other tips convey the specialized genre knowledge of information graphics, such as choosing a pie chart when you want to see the relationship between a whole and its parts. Some tips come from a combination of Gestalt, genre-based, and research principles. For example, keeping graph areas proportional to the data avoids a distortion that arises from our perception of the graph's size combined with our genre knowledge that visual size is usually proportional to the data results. For important information about the limits of these visuals, especially their potential for stereotyping and distortion, see Chapter 3.

Do plan to include images or information graphics if your genre permits. Readers focus on them right away. See Chapter 4 for likely choices for particular genres. Many ready-made images—such as clip art and stock photography—are now widely available to incorporate into collegiate writing. Charts can be drawn with graph paper or created in word processing, presentation, or spreadsheet software. Be aware that research papers and reports have very specific rules for creating, placing, and labeling information graphics. These vary somewhat by field, so consult with your instructor about requirements.

General tips

Here are some general tips for adding images or information graphics to your document.

Fit the picture to your purpose and audience

Casual readers or viewers of presentations often need informal, relatively simple information graphics with color and interesting images while scientists and professors will expect careful, rather more complex graphics without extraneous detail, or ***chartjunk*** (Tufte, *Visual Display* 107). Consult Chapter 4 to help plan.

Make a point with each visual— make that point clear in the text

- Use callouts from the text to the visual: "See the chart below." "In the following table, . . ." Or more formally, "In the next scene, the woman's gaze is toward the viewer (Figure 2)."

Tell readers what they're looking at

- Include labels and informative titles.
- Write captions for news photos.
- If you have many images or information graphics, consider numbering them, as Figure 1, Figure 2— or simply 1, 2, and so on. See format guidelines for research papers for extended examples.

Make the picture the right size

- Test it in the setting. If the picture will be reduced, try making a photocopy at a smaller size to see if everything is still legible. If the picture will be viewed from a distance, have a helper test that it is clear at that distance.
- Learn to resize digital images without changing the proportions. Otherwise they will look distorted. See your software's instructions or ask for help with this important step.

Make the relevant features stand out

- Use figure-ground contrast and clear shading.
- Give enough visual context to orient readers, but also help them focus.

- Crop photos to focus on the important parts.
- Choose the most relevant data points.
- Cue readers with an arrow or other mark, but don't clutter up the picture with extra marks.

Place the picture as soon after the relevant text as possible—on the same page or a facing page

> NOTE: Some research paper and report formats require that all tables, images, and information graphics—the last two formally referred to as figures—be placed at the back of the paper. Check the requirements with your instructor.

Frame the picture—and titles and labels—with a small buffer of white space

- Some genres, like newsletters and brochures, allow you to run a column of text around an image or graphic.
- In other genres, you simply place graphics "in line" between paragraphs of text.

Make sure objects are large enough for color to show up

Human factors research suggests that an object has to be the size of a 36-point *O* to carry color (Coe 151):

Figure 7.1 Letter "O" in 36-point Times New Roman

For the same reason, you should avoid color for tiny patterns. If you color text, make whole words the same color.

Don't distort the meaning

- On charts, make the baseline clear.
- Keep graph areas proportional to the data.

- On maps, give the scale.
- Don't manipulate photos or other images used for their informative or documentary content.
- Consider the ethical implications before you manipulate images intended to support mood or theme.

Give credit

- Put a source line below images and information graphics that you reproduce from other sources.
- Check the copyright of graphics and know whether your use is *fair use*. *Fair use* allows writers, editors, and others to use the copyrighted works of others, within certain limits, without asking permission of the copyright owner. In general, a single reproduction of a copyrighted image for educational purposes is considered fair use. Multiple copies, especially for profit, generally require permission. Factual information is less restricted than creative works, including images, for which permission may be required.
- If you collect the data and create the graphics yourself, make that clear.

Tips for adding images

For images that create a mood, consider who will respond to the image and who may feel excluded

- Images have an ethos. You may like the mood, but does it include your audience as well?

Remember that clip art and stock photography may reinforce gender, racial, and ethnic stereotypes

- Try some of the analysis questions in Chapter 3.

For portfolio covers or poem settings, create collages of ready-made images

- Use proximity and other Gestalt principles to create associations among disparate elements.

136

Treat images that are the subject of an analysis as if they were information graphics

If you write a lengthy analysis of an ad or other image, reproduce it as part of your argument. You may also need to copy important details (perhaps enlarged) and place them separately near your discussion of each detail. Label the image, give your source, and use callouts to make clear which areas you are discussing.

Tips for adding information graphics

Choose the right graphic for your data and rhetorical purpose.[1]

Table 7.2 Deciding on a type of graphic

If your reader needs to	Choose
get an overview	outline, list, table, or flowchart
compare options or exact quantities	table
see how a whole is divided into parts	pie chart
compare amounts in different categories	bar chart, column chart
see change over time	line graph, area chart
examine patterns of many data points	scatterplot

Realize that technical line drawings can be more informative than photographs

Drawings are more selective and can help readers focus on the structure and relevant features.

Use good visual formatting

- Don't overload any one table, graph, or chart.
- Keep gridlines to the minimum that your readers need for understanding.

137

- Remember that color can highlight but also distract—if you are allowed to use color, do so with care, to make trends and distinctions in data clear.
- Avoid putting different textures together—that's distracting and uninformative.
- Use shading to show trend or ordering.
- Make the different variables visually distinctive, as in the following scatterplot:

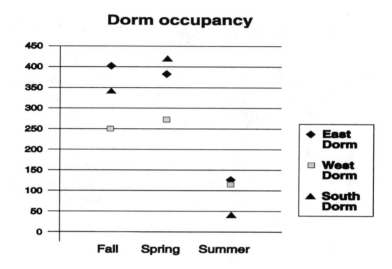

Figure 7.3 A scatterplot with different variables

The different shapes let readers track the information for the three dorms. For example, South Dorm (triangles) had the highest occupancy in spring and the lowest in summer.

In tables, ensure that like items read down (Day 62)

NOT

Table 7.4 Imaginary Pebbles 1			
	Sample 1	Sample 2	Sample 3
size	6.5 mm	8 mm	17 mm
color	red	magenta	turquoise
weight	0.5 mg	0.7 mg	6.2 mg

BUT

Table 7.5 Imaginary Pebbles 2			
Sample	Size (mm)	Color	Weight (mg)
1	6.5	red	0.5
2	8.	magenta	0.7
3	17.	turquoise	6.2

The second table is tidier. More importantly, it helps readers to compare similar categories, like size.

Exercises

1. Take the quotation, poem, or scrap of graffiti that you set in type in Chapter 6. Now add an image to the setting: a photograph, a drawing, an illustration from clip art or the Web (give credit to your source on the back of the page). Compare the type-only setting and the one with the image. What is the difference in tone? In emphasis? What does that tell you about images? Try two or three versions, and ask others to give you feedback about their experience of the different versions.

Notes

[1]The following resources offer more detailed advice for choosing a graph type: William Horton, "Pictures Please—Presenting Information Visually," *Techniques for Technical Communicators*, ed. Carol M. Barnum and Saul Carliner (New York: Macmillan, 1993), pp. 187-218; Stephen M. Kosslyn, "Visual Table of Contents" and "Choosing a Graph Format," *Elements of Graph Design* (New York: Freeman, 1994), pp. x-xi and 19-61; Charles Kostelnick and David D. Roberts, "Data Displays," *Designing Visual Language: Strategies for Professional Communicators* (Boston: Allyn & Bacon, 1998), pp. 263-312.

CHAPTER 8

Putting It Together: Sample Documents

This chapter contains several sample documents designed or re-designed by students. All were enrolled in a visual communication seminar as part of a graduate program in professional communication, which emphasizes writing and rhetoric. Some of the students had experience in graphic or interface design while others were just beginning to think visually. In some examples, the documents are "before" and "after" versions. In others, only a final design is shown. Some of the students' own comments are included in the discussion.

As they worked, they conferred with us, their instructors, about demonstrating principles of visual communication. They considered their audiences. They tried out different ideas. They revised. They struggled to comprehend new software. They learned about production. Above all, they taught us—about technology, creativity, and fruitful collaboration.

Look at these samples as a source of questions as well as answers. Examine them in light of the guidelines in Chapters 4, 5, 6, and 7. What choices were made? What could have been done differently?

Poem

Keena Hamilton typeset this well-known poem by William Wordsworth to demonstrate its expressive, lyrical qualities. Like many of the samples here, it went through several versions. This version is based on her final design. The text is aligned along the right margin. This striking choice supports its expressive purpose. Students of Wordsworth will also note that the original 12-line poem is here broken into 16 lines. Keena employs several techniques from Chapters 5 and 6. All elements are right-aligned, so nothing distracts. There are strong contrasts, such as the white space on the left versus the lines of the text to the right. The script drop capital *S* contrasts with the body type in size, weight, and slant. The poem's font seems ordinary but has unusual touches. Look at the delicate angled serifs, the tall ascenders that "reach to the sky" (as in *dwelt*), and the looped *k*. To keep the text legible and not crowd those tall ascenders, Keena used ample leading (space between lines).

She dwelt among th'
untrodden ways
Beside the
springs of Dove:
A maid whom there were
none to praise
And very few to love.
A violet by a mossy stone
Half-hidden from the eye!
Fair as a star when only one
Is shining in the sky!
She lived unknown,
and few could know
When Lucy ceased to be;
But she is in her grave, and oh!
The difference to me.
—William Wordsworth

Figure 8.1 Visual interpretation of a poem

Resume

Resumes benefit from good visual organization and emphasis. The less experience you have, the more you need good organization in the writing and the layout. Esther Revis-Wagner created both of these resumes, based on the experiences of a fictional person. In the revision, she strove for visual emphasis, well grouped blocks of text, clear visual layers, a strong left alignment, and an overall coherence of type and structure.

Ophelia Roberts

661 Beach Island Avenue
Seabreeze, SC 29444
(843)888-9444
ruberta@clemson.edu

Education: Bachelor of Science, Management Sciences, Clemson University, Expected Graduation Date: May 2002
Relative Coursework: Human Resources Development, Computer Science, Marketing, Transportation
Senior Research Project: Stress in the Business Environment

Work Experience:

Resident Assistant, Clemson University; Sanders Dormitory
Monitored a residence hall.

Sales clerk, Macy's Department Store
Worked in the Credit Department, Gift wrap, and Men's wear.

Bank Teller, First Union Bank of S.C.

Waitress, Scoopie Doo Ice Cream Shoppe
Waited on customers.

Hospital Volunteer, University Hospital, Charleston, S.C.
Delivered flowers, delivered prescriptions, delivered patients to their rooms after admission

Special Interests: Lady Tiger Basketball
Logistics Club
Gun Club

REFERENCES AVAILABLE UPON REQUEST

Computer Software Skills: Microsoft Word (version 3.1), Java Script, Microsoft Excel (version 2.0), C++ Programming, Power Point, HTML Programming (see my web page at http://ruberta.com), Basic Programming

Figure 8.2 Poorly organized and developed resume

143

Ophelia Roberts

ruberta@clemson.edu

661 Beach Island Avenue
Seabreeze, SC 29444
(843)555-9444

Education   Bachelor of Science in Management Sciences, Clemson University
Anticipated Graduation Date, May 2002

Relative Coursework

Computer Science	Human Resource Development
International Marketing	Marketing and the World Wide Web
Transportation and Logistics	International Trade and ISO 9000

Senior Research Project

Stress Management in the Business Environment- A semester-long study
of methods and practices corporations utilize to help their
employees alleviate the stresses inside and outside the workplace.

Objective   To obtain a summer internship with an international corporation where I can
utilize my marketing and web development experience.

Work Experience

Resident Assistant, *Clemson University,* 2000-2001

Coordinated activities and programs for residents in a dormitory.
Moderated interpersonal disputes between roommates and
neighbors. Maintained decorum. Acted as a liaison between
residents and University officials.

Sales Clerk, *Macy's: Credit Department, Gift Wrap, and Men's Ware,* 1998-2000

Balanced a cash drawer on a daily basis. Handled customer
complaints. Inventoried stock.

Bank Teller, *First Union Bank of South Carolina,* 2001

Reconciled teller drawer daily. Assisted customers with account
balancing. Covered vacation schedules between four branch banks.

Hospital Volunteer, *University Hospital,* 1995-1998

Delivered flowers to patients in their rooms. Couriered narcotic
prescriptions from the hospital pharmacy to the nurses' stations.
Escorted patients to their rooms upon admission.
Awarded *Volunteer With the Most Hours Served* four consecutive years.

Computer Software Skills   Visit <http://ruberta.com> for examples of my work with

Power Point	HTML	Microsoft Word	Microsoft Excel

Special Interests

Lady Tiger Basketball- Organized student road trips to away games.
Gun Club- Participated in Intercollegiate club competitions.
Logistics Club- Student member of local national organization.

Reverences Available Upon Request

Figure 8.3 Revised resume

144

Logo

Logos are inviting projects but often difficult to design. Christopher Lohr created both of these logos for a fictional propellor supply company to demonstrate some of the hazards. The original logo is cluttered and distracting. In addition to being crowded and hard to read, the typefaces combine poorly with each other, and the image wrongly suggests that the company deals in airplanes rather than in custom propellers. The revised logo is readable and appropriate. The image of the propellor focuses on the nature of the business. The typefaces have the same lines as the image.

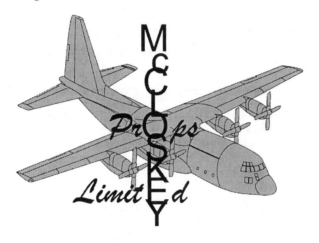

Figure 8.4 Overgeneralized and cluttered logo

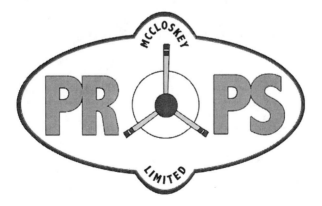

Figure 8.5 Focused, "clear" logo

145

Flyer

The original was an actual flyer hung at a major university advertising the meeting of the Speech and Communications Club. It was meant to grab the attention of all passersby, even though the target group was speech majors. The purpose of the new flyer is the same, but it employs different fonts and point sizes to attract the notice of passersby. Rebecca Pope redesigned the flyer and provided these notes:

Original:

- The whole text is centered and dull.
- All text is in the same sans serif font, with no variations in size or thickness, giving all the text equal importance.
- Overuse of exclamation points actually detracts from emphasis.
- Equal spacing between all items fails to draw the eye down the page.
- Visually boring.

Revision:

- Large, exciting font gets the attention of speech majors immediately.
- Use of three fonts creates visual contrast and draws the eye to important items.
- Change in font size draws eye down the page and gives the more important items visual precedence.
- Thick black lines meeting in bottom right corner draw the eye down through the information.

(Original courtesy of the Speech & Communication Studies Department, Clemson University)

Speech and Communications Club Meeting!!!

**Wednesday 5:00
Daniel 413**

We will be planning our trip to the University of Georgia Graduate School!

All Majors Welcome. Speech Majors BE THERE!!

Figure 8.6 Original flyer

Interested in **GRADUATE** school?

   Like going on random **ROAD TRIPS**?

   Just **WANT TO GET OUT** of this town?

If you can answer **YES** to any of these questions, join us!

What: Speech and Communications Club Meeting

When: Wednesday, October 28

Where: Daniel Hall 413

Agenda: We will be planning our trip to the University of Georgia Gradute School.

Who: Everyone is welcome to join us. Speech majors, **be there** or else!

Figure 8.7 Revised flyer

Proposal

Myra Whittemore is both the author and the designer of this proposal for a local history project. She knew that her readers, members of the South Carolina Humanities Commission, were interested in funding small projects. These contribute to the state's historical and literary life, yet must also benefit a diverse group of citizens—in this case the community of Wadmalaw Island, Myra's home. Visuals add interest and a focal point. They can also help to show that the proposer is committed to the project and shares the values of the Humanities Commission. Myra decided to add two graphics: 1) a table (generated in a spreadsheet) for her budget, and 2) a clip art image that evoked the locale and expressed the benefits of her project.

A note about the illustration: Wadmalaw Island's history and the natural setting of palmettos and live oaks recall the Old South. Yet, as Myra found, commonly available clip art may suggest an indirect nostalgia for the former white-dominated plantation culture. She rejected an evocative illustration of an older African-American working man as potentially condescending.

The image that she eventually chose, a spreading tree, does not represent anything particular to coastal South Carolina. Nor did it reproduce as well as others she could have used. However, it does not have negative connotations. And Myra found that she could use the image to convey the theme of "One Grant, Many Outcomes," labeling the tree's branches with the many benefits that her project would generate.

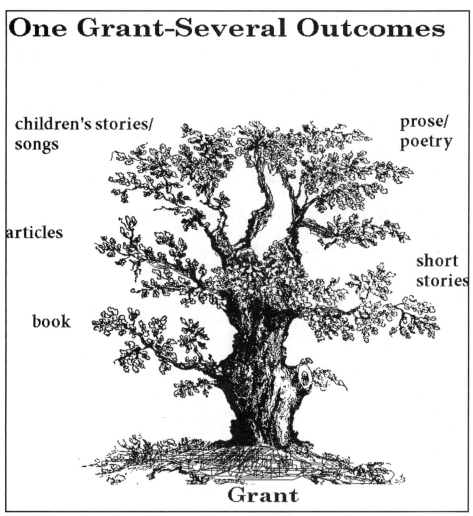

Figure 8.8 Visual proposal

Presentation slides

These slides are visual support for a short talk about engineering as a career. The talk is aimed at high school students and college freshmen. The first versions show many of the problems in creating legible, interesting slides, such as patterned backgrounds, too much text, and inconsistent choices of font. The revisions are not only more legible, but through a consistent, dynamic layout, are also more interesting. The slides and comments are by Ryan Keith.

The title slide (Figure 8.9) has a patterned background that reduces the contrast for the type. The revision (Figure 8.10) creates greater contrast with the foreground, groups related information, and uses left alignment. A second slide from the presentation (Figure 8.11) selects key phrases, bullets the items, and restricts the fonts to one serif and one sans serif.

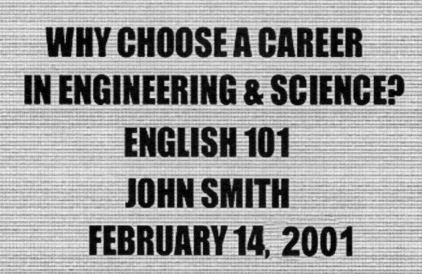

Figure 8.9 Poor title slide

Figure 8.10 Revised title slide

Various
fields in engineering

- Traditional

- Hot new fields

- Areas of Specialization

Figure 8.11 Slide with key phrases

Web pages

Web pages, like presentation slides, offer so many design options that it is easy to overwhelm the reader. Remember that Web readers scan a page from link to link, searching for the next interesting place to go. Deb Staed, who teaches students and faculty how to make interesting, well-designed Web pages and multimedia presentations, created this typical homepage (Figure 8.12) and revised it to be more legible (Figure 8.13). The first version has a distracting background that makes the slender type hard to read (see Figure 2.3 in Chapter 2 for discussion of this kind of problem). The images, the band of flowers and the sun, have blank backgrounds and are not integrated into the page's overall visual field. Nor are there any links, so the reader may feel this page is a "dead end." The revision has a simple white background, so that the type and images stand out. The repeated suns are used as bullets to create a consistent theme for the links, which lead viewers further into the site. The whole is organized but still sprightly and full of the creator's personality.

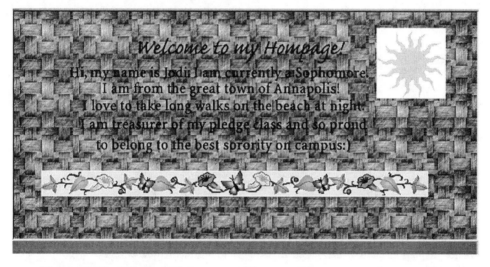

Figure 8.12 Original Web page with poor figure-ground separation

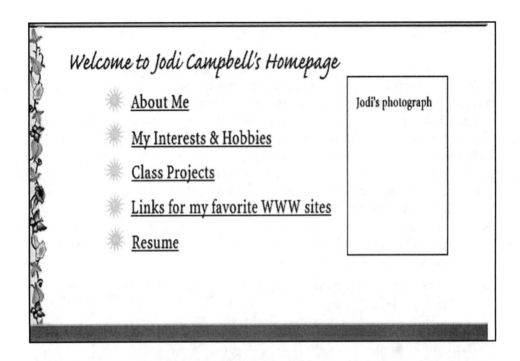

Figure 8.13 Revised Web page with high contrast and strong alignment

The following Web page (Figure 8.14) was created by Sarah Weathers for a company that offers cleaning services. Based loosely on the inverted-L format, with a contents bar at the left, the site has features that break up the "blocky" or squarish look normally associated with the inverted-L format. For example, the shaded triangle in the logo (colored blue in Sarah's version) cuts through the letters of the company's name. The two areas of the logo, colored blue and white, echo each other, reversing background and foreground and unifying the image. The contrasts created, as well as the unusual but clear shapes, add a dynamic quality to the page.

Figure 8.14 Sarah Weather's CeilBrite Web page

Image Poem

Another application of unusual shapes to direct attention and add interest occurs in the next sample, an image poem by Angela Davis (Figure 8.15). Angela began this project when her class was assigned Exercise 1 from Chapter 7. Created as a poster, the document reverses normal expectations of reading and viewing. The background, a photograph of the Eiffel Tower shown from pedestrian level, divides the page into vivid darker and lighter areas. The darkest area, the bottom, creates the greatest contrast with the large words in reversed type, so attention is drawn there. Decreasing size is used to direct readers to read from bottom to top, and several words use the edges of the page and the image as anchors in a "step" movement upward. There is a punning relationship between the words and the image, too.

155

Figure 8.15 Angela Davis' Poster

Brochure

The brochure on the following pages was created by Michelle Slater and Parker Smith in order recruit new students for Clemson's MA in Professional Communication program by advertising the kinds of careers graduates could pursue. Creating and reading a "tri-fold" brochure like this one takes a fair amount of imagination because, like Web pages, you have to think carefully about the "navigation" system for the brochure. How will the user of a brochure interact with its folding?

This brochure has a traditional format: an 8.5" by 11" page folded in thirds, called a "tri-fold." Because of the folding, there are six panels, three on the front page and three on the back. After the page has been folded, the front panel stands alone and attracts the reader inside. On opening, the reader then typically sees the inside "flap" and one of the inside panels, then the rest of the inside. A reader may then scan the inner panels as one cohesive page. The back panel usually contains contact information, such as the mailing and Web site addresses shown in Figure 8.17.

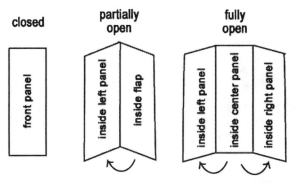

Figure 8.16 Opening panels of a tri-fold brochure

Note how the authors used font size and shading to emphasize the names of the careers on each panel, except for the front or cover panel. Notice also how they divided each panel into two columns and made very subtle use of the same font shading for the pull quotes that they used for the large headers. The effect here is to pull readers into each panel, encouraging them to read more closely. Note that we have added labels to each panel in order to make the brochure's navigation easier to follow.

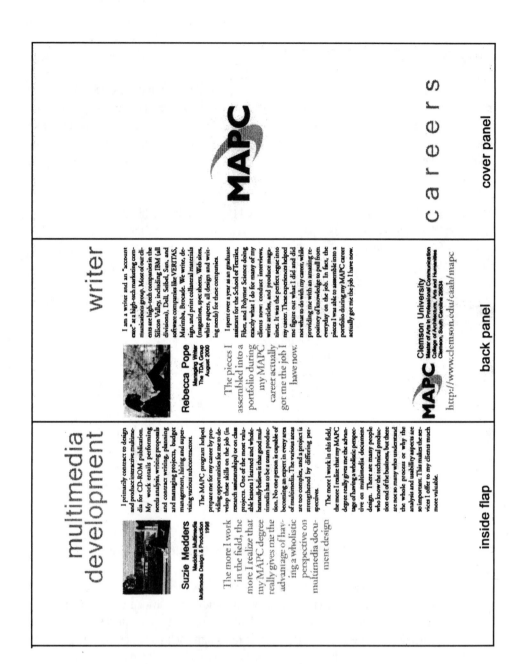

MAPC

careers

cover panel

---

writer

Rebecca Pope
Managing Writer
The TDA Group
August 2000

I am a writer and an "account exec" at a high-tech marketing communications group. Most of our clients are high-tech companies in the Silicon Valley, including IBM (all divisions), Dell, Seibel, Sun, and software companies like VERITAS, Marimba, Brocade. We write, design, and print collateral materials (magazines, spec sheets, Web sites, white papers, all design and writing needs) for these companies.

I spent over a year as an graduate assistant for the School of Textiles, Fiber, and Polymer Science doing exactly what I do for many of my clients now: conduct interviews, write articles, and produce magazines. It was the perfect segue into my career. These experiences helped me figure out what I did and did not want to do with my career, while providing me with an amazing repository of knowledge to pull from everyday on the job. In fact, the pieces I was able to assemble into a portfolio during my MAPC career actually got me the job I have now.

The pieces I assembled into a portfolio during my MAPC career actually got me the job I have now.

MAPC Clemson University
Master of Arts in Professional Communication
College of Architecture, Arts, and Humanities
Clemson, South Carolina 29634
http://www.clemson.edu/caah/mapc

back panel

---

multimedia development

Suzie Medders
Medders Multimedia
1998
Multimedia Design & Production

I primarily contract to design and produce interactive multimedia for CD-ROM publication. My work entails performing needs analysis, writing proposals and contract writing, planning and managing projects, budget management, hiring and supervising various subcontractors.

The MAPC program helped prepare me for my career by providing opportunities for me to develop these skills on the job (in research assistantship) or on class projects. One of the most valuable lessons I learned and wholeheartedly believe is that good multimedia has to be a team production. No one person is capable of becoming an expert in every area of multimedia. The various areas are too complex, and a project is strengthened by differing perspectives.

The more I work in the field, the more I realize that my MAPC degree really gives me the advantage of having a wholistic perspective on multimedia document design

The more I work in this field, the more I realize that my MAPC degree really gives me the advantage of having a wholistic perspective on multimedia document design. There are many people who know the technical production end of the business, but there are not so many who understand the whole process or why the analysis and usability aspects are so important. This makes the services I offer to my clients much more valuable.

inside flap

Figure 8.17 Page one of a tri-fold brochure

Figure 8.18 Page two of a tri-fold brochure

Newsletters

Parker Smith created this newsletter by redesigning an actual newsletter as a class assignment. Parker's redesigned newsletter (Figure 8.19) has an asymmetrical, yet balanced layout. (See Chapter 5 and Figure 5.5 for more discussion of balance.) "Squint" at this layout. The two darker portions of the page, the title Livewire and the left-hand column, should stand out. They are balanced against each other. The title, aligned flush right, has bold black letters that contrast well against the white background. The title is smaller but more dramatic than the left column, which is medium gray. Thus the two sections are balanced in value and tonal density, that is, the area covered by ink. The layout also has plenty of figure-ground contrast, using ample white space around these darker areas as well as to set off the two right-hand text columns.

Other features help to define parts of the page and also to unify the look. The different types of information on the page have different visual emphasis and treatment. The gray column on the left contains routine scheduling information. The two white columns both contain news and editorial content. The small graphics like the Web (behind the title), the book, and the envelope are somewhat casual line drawings. They are consistent with each other in tone and style. Thus, while they are different images, their common treatment pulls the different areas together, draws the reader into the page, and cues each new part of the page.

In this issue

Students Present Papers
Summer GAs and Fall TAs
MAPC email
Southern Circuit News

http://www.clemson.edu/caah/engl/mapc/index.htm

Core Course Offerings

In light of the many rumors and stories flying around the department about the future of the MAPC core courses, We at MAPC News felt it only fitting to set the record straight. According to Dr. Charney, every core couse will not be offered every semester as the rumor has said, but the plan is to offer as many core courses as possible as well as a wide variety of electives in an effort to appease as many people as possible. The following is the plan for course offerings in the next academic year, 1999-2000, which may be altered depend-ing on the newly hired incoming professors.

Fall
833 Rhetoric of Science
851 Professional Writing
852 Rhetoric and Prof. Comm.
853 Visual Communication
854 Teaching Professional Writing
885 Composition Theory

Spring
801 Composition Theory Seminar
838 International Communication
850 Research
853 Visual Communication
856 Workplace Communciation

Summer I
836 Digital Publishing

Summer II
832 Special Topics

Receptions for Potential MAPC Faculty

The MAPC program is lucky enough to be interviewing several extraordinary candidates who could potentially fill several open positions in the faculty. Currently the department has several spots open for professors, including the Pearce Chair, and several visiting candidates interested in coming to Clemson. The department hosted a reception at the home of Dr. Beth Daniell for a rhetoric and composition canditidate. The reception is scheduled for Sunday, January 24. All MAPC students were invited to attend and meet the prospective professor. As with all of the receptions scheduled for the future, students are invited to come meet these visitors, because, as Dr. Howard said, our input is just as important as that of the other faculty. So get involved by attending several of these functions. Watch your e-mail for specific dates of the visits or e-mail Dr. Morrissey at: lmorris@hubcap.clemson. edu for more information.

February Southern Circuit

The South Carolina Arts Commission, with support from local sponsors, announces the presentation of Southern Circuit's The Farm, a film documentary set in America's most infamous maximum security prison. The one of the film's directors, Liz Garbus, will be present the night of the showing, February 1, 1999 at 7:30 PM in Vickery Hall Auditorium. Admission is free.

MAPC E-Mail List

Dr. Howard is in the process of updating the MAPC E-mail list. If you are not on this list and would like to be, please contact Dr. Howard (tharon@clemson.edu). Here is just a little reminder of for what the list is intended, excepted from the original e-mail we all received. The MAPC e-mail list (MAPC@hubcap.clemson.edu) serves as a discussion group "to promote conver-sations of interest to students, faculty, staff and alumni

(continued on back)

Figure 8.19 Opening page of a sample newsletter

CHAPTER 9

Learning More about Visual Communication

This guide gives a great deal of advice—prescriptions for good visual communication, if you will. However, the advice is just that, good counsel, not law writ in stone. Part of being informed about visual communication is to recognize that it has a history and cultural context, just as rhetoric does. Thus its terms are not universal or timeless but always in the process of being adapted and contested. The document format that is perfectly acceptable for one instructor or work supervisor may be rejected by another. What looks appropriate, innovative, or attractive at one time is judged improper, dated, or dull at another. When you ask readers to give you feedback about the look of your document, they may focus on completely different aspects of it. The contradictions do not mean that readers' acceptance of a document's look is random or whimsical. In fact, there are a number of cultural circumstances that help explain advice about visual design—and explain why it may be contradictory.

This guide also has a context. It draws heavily on a few movements, theories, and practices about visuals: modernist aesthetics, semiotics, ideological criticism, cognitive psychology, and technical communication, as well as rhetoric.

This chapter summarizes some influences on visual communication as a subject. It attempts one answer to the question: Where do ideas about the ads, logos, magazines, manuals, Web sites, and other print and electronic communications come from? The answer is found in the social, technological, and intellectual contexts of published documents and public communications—the history of their making and the experiences of their makers.

Books, articles, and Internet sites about print and Web design abound. The bibliography lists a number of these, and more appear every day. Many are excellent. Often the advice is phrased as "Do this, don't do that." (This guide makes similar pronouncements.) Such certainty is in fact part of our prevailing assumptions about the ethos of the visual, its intuitiveness or transparency. However, consider the source and context of your information. Here are some aspects of visual communication to explore further.

Graphic design: the text as image

Published documents have long incorporated the specialized knowledge of **graphic design**. Graphic design encompasses the entire process of **delivery**, or to use a publishing term, **production**: arranging text and visuals on pages or screens, plus choosing type, color, and details of paper, ink, and binding (for print documents) or platform and interface (for screen documents). Even publications that seem to be entirely textual have been visually designed. In rhetorical terms, graphic design makes use of "typography, illustration, photography, and printing for purposes of persuasion, information, or instruction" (Schriver 79). In aesthetic terms, graphic design brings "structural order and visual form to printed communications" (Meggs xiii). Printed and now electronic mass communication—posters, advertising, public relations (including corporate identity programs and logos), books, magazines, and multimedia interfaces—are major areas in which graphic design is applied.

The large, many-faceted 20th-century artistic and architectural movement called modernism and its successor, postmodernism, are especially important. The legacy of these very different approaches to design is not static, but always being challenged and adapted.

Modernism and graphic design

In the late 19th and early 20th-centuries, European visual artists' responses to rapid technological, scientific, and social changes were "a series of creative revolutions" that together are called modernism (Meggs 238). Modernist ideas and values have profoundly influenced the look of communications, especially since World War II. In graphic design, the most influential form of modernism has been the International Typographic Style, or Swiss style, that is evident in everything from our highway and airport signs to informational brochures, corporate logos, and international symbols for Olympic events. From modernist aesthetics comes the emphasis on **function, simplicity of form, universality with objectivity, and intuition** that is featured in much advice about the visual design of documents.

Function. "Form follows function," the byword of modern architecture, also characterizes modernist graphic design. Reflecting the values of machines and speed, designers reexamined everything from furniture to page layouts to discern how people encountered and used the material objects of their lives. Those uses gave rise to the forms of the objects. As Karen Schriver has noted, this interplay of form and function, between the design and the user's needs, is rhetorical (84). Modernist designers also sought to unify text and form, so that the look of the letters, words, and pages reflected the values of the language (Kostelnick, "Typographical Design" 10). That is, the look of the text was in part a functional reflection of its meaning. The same emphasis on function led to a focus on economy and simplicity of form.

Simplicity. If a design element is not functional, it is unnecessary. Modernist painters like Pablo Picasso and Piet Mondrian and architects like Walter Gropius saw the world in terms of abstract shapes. Modernist designers of posters, books, and magazines like Lazslo Moholy-Nagy and Jan Tschichold cleared the page and began to work with geometric areas of white space, lines, photographs of machines and tools with their abstract forms, and blocks of text. Type designers created many new *sans serif* typefaces, which were cleaner and simpler in shape than serif types. Herbert Bayer of the Bauhaus design school even declared that it was redundant to use both upper- and lowercase letters, so that he omitted capital letters in his pages (Meggs 294).

The drive to simplify also carried over to signs and symbolic communication. The development of *icons* can be traced to experiments like Otto Neurath's Isotype, a system of pictographs that simplified statistical data (Meggs 303-4). The human form was also simplified in these efforts. In the area of maps, Henry C. Beck's map for the London Underground, created in 1933, presented a simplified, brightly colored diagram instead of a conventional map that was faithful to geographic distances (Meggs 304). This famous map became the pattern for subway maps all over the world.

Universality and objectivity. Reducing forms, including the human form, to basic shared elements is one way to eliminate the differences that divide people and obscure their common goals. The Isotype goal of a "'world language without words'" was to aid public understanding of "issues relating to housing, health, and economics" (Meggs 303). A universal system to reach all people across languages and cultures has been the goal of many modernist-influenced systems of transportation and event signs, from the U.S. Interstate highway system to the international symbols in airports to Olympic event icons.

Because it was a response to and often a celebration of science, technology, and industrialization, modernism also values objectivity. In particular, modernists assume that the perceptual capabilities of eye and brain are shared by all humans, so that there is a universal response to visual communication (Kostelnick, "Cultural Adaptation" 182-83). The principles of Gestalt psychology reflect this assumption. So does some document design research, such as legibility and readability studies. However, even type is not culturally neutral, as Robin Kinross has shown (135-36).

Intuition. Modernist ideas have not only influenced the look but also the process of designing documents and the source of visual ideas. Much design advice counsels to use your intuition—just going with "what looks right." That advice can be traced back to the Bauhaus, which privileged the intuition of individuals and cultures as the source of truth and good design (Kostelnick, "Typographical Design" 19). One effect—at least on those who have not been educated in architecture, art, or design—has been to obscure the roots of the very principles that have so influenced the look of communications.

Modernism in sum. The values of modernist design appear everywhere in guidelines for visual communication. Function and simplicity of form have been embodied in tenets about analyzing the reader, unifying the tone of text and type, using white space, employing grid structures, creating balanced but not rigidly symmetrical layouts, employing Gestalt principles of perception, and striving for clarity of communication as well as a restrained expressiveness. These and many other precepts based on modernist ideas retain their power and usefulness today. Yet there are contradictions inherent in modernism, especially in the simultaneous quest for objectivity and intuition. These principles also require assumptions and choices that may not suit the rhetorical situation. For example, the belief that humans respond universally to visual forms disregards the importance of culture and experience—genre knowledge, for example—in our understanding of even quite simple visual elements.

After modernism. Starting in the 1970's, architects and designers have challenged the more troubling assumptions of modernism. The many varied responses are usually called *postmodernism*. In contrast to the modernist's ideal of universal design, postmodernists recognize the political, social, and historical meanings of design forms (Meggs 446). They call attention to the very limits of the forms they employ, and often use design to critique and contextualize particular visual styles. Because postmodernism acknowledges the social and political settings of documents and other objects, ideological critics have applied its ideas to everything from maps to interior design. (Barton and Barton, "Ideology" 49-50; Lupton, "The Bathroom" 25). In contrast to modernism's simplicity (and therefore its tendency to exclude), postmodernism embraces differences, even to the point of chaos. Harking back to earlier 20th-century art movements like Dada, postmodernism also acknowledges the visual impact of mass and consumer culture, blending ads and comic book images irreverently with reproductions of acknowledged masterpieces, like the Mona Lisa (Appignanesi and Garratt 32). Postmodernist designers value play, complexity, randomness, visual punning and a self-reflexive irony. Collage, *grunge* typography—"ugly" or "subversive" fonts—and "retro" design all share a postmodern visual sensibility (Williams, *Blip* 9).

Other influences on visual communication

Outside the arts themselves, other developments have influenced the dialogue about visual communication in documents. Some of these take up both the interpretation and the production of documents. Others primarily concern interpretation, especially on the reading of images in advertising, the media, and governmental publications. The emphasis in the following sections is on influential and accessible works in each strand.

Information graphics and visual problem solving

In the physical sciences, technology, social sciences, and applied arts, the production of visuals is an issue that has influenced the discussion about visual communication. Information graphics is concerned with the clear, accurate production and interpretation of scientific, technical, and numerical research data. Until the introduction of personal computers, information graphics were typically the domain of specialized technical illustrators. Illustrators made a variety of charts, figures, and other illustrations for scientific and engineering journals, but also popular magazines and newspapers. When computers (and calculators) put graphing tools into the hands of researchers themselves, interest in the design of information graphics moved out of the illustrator's craft and into wider discussion.

In the applied arts and technology, architects, urban planners, designers, and landscape architects have always needed some drawing skills. While these skills have typically been honed by a craft approach, through design and (for some) mechanical drawing courses, a more creative approach has evolved since the 1960's. Visual problem solving allies psychology, sketching, problem-solving techniques, and systems thinking.

Information graphics. The production of clear, accessible charts and graphs to illustrate numerical data has had a relatively long craft tradition of "how-to" advice (Schriver 81). That situation changed with the 1983 publication of *The Visual Display of Quantitative Information* by Edward R. Tufte. Tufte offered a theory, history, and aesthetics of data graphics. *Visual Display* has had great influence in the sciences, technical communication, and commercial as well as desktop publishing. Tufte's principles, as well as the design of his several books, place him philosophically and aesthetically with modernism (Kostelnick, "Cultural Adaptation" 191), although some have noted a split between modernist and postmodernist sensibility (Barton and Barton, "Postmodernism" 256). However, he has been most criticized for ignoring the rhetorical situation in which information graphics are created and viewed. For example, Tufte's analysis of the Challenger disaster points out that the graphics prepared to show that

167

the launch should be delayed were faulty (*Visual Explanations* 40). Lee Brasseur argues that better graphics would not by themselves have changed the outcome, as Tufte has suggested (Brasseur 343).

The rhetorical context of information graphics has received attention from geographer Mark Monmonier. In the area of medical journalism and illustration, Sean McNaughton, a reporter and information graphic artist, has written a case history of a complex, two-day feature article on prostate cancer for the *Boston Globe* (McNaughton 488).

Visual problem solving. Many professions require creativity, and one contemporary approach to enhancing creativity is visual problem solving. This movement has been fueled to some degree by Rudolf Arnheim's interdisciplinary approach in *Visual Thinking* (1969), drawing on psychology as well as the visual arts (McKim 199). The study of mind and brain continues to influence this movement, including studies of the brain's hemispheres that have opposed visual and verbal processing as well as the discussion of different "intelligences" such as spatial intelligence by Howard Gardner and others. Because it seeks to enhance individual and group creativity, visual problem solving also draws on the human potential movements of the late 20th-century. This literature typically mixes abstract visual puzzles (for example, from the Gestaltists) with word puzzles, design problems, rapid sketching exercises, explanations of brain function, and maxims for releasing creativity. In addition to Arnheim, the writing of Edward De Bono, such as *New Think*, is influential here. This movement also renewed interest in the drawing techniques of Kimon Nicolaides. Another significant mainstream drawing book is Betty Edwards' *Drawing on the Right Side of the Brain*. The influence of visual problem solving extends well beyond architecture and design into fields like management, software engineering, and multimedia design.

Information visualization. Computer technology makes possible intricately detailed two- and three-dimensional displays. That capability has accelerated interest in new types of information graphics and research into visual representations of data. A relatively new field called *information visualization* "applies vision research to practical problems of data analysis," combining psychological research and engineering (Ware 33). This complex field connects with the work of Tufte, as well as visual problem solving, human factors, and usability studies. A good starting point is the first chapter of *Readings in Information Visualization: Using Vision to Think.* With Jacques Bertin's dictum, "Graphics is the visual means of resolving logical problems," as their motto, authors Stuart A. Card, Jock D. Mackinlay, and Ben Shneiderman give solid explanations and accessible examples.

Semiotics, cultural criticism, and visual literacy

The abundance of images around us has prompted intellectual debate about the way that they construct our ideas. The images presented in the media, as well as the visual environment—consumer objects, interior design, buildings—of our everyday life are the subject of much analysis and critique. As Ellen Lupton and J. Abbott Miller have remarked, "the very omnipresence of products and media" is "a socializing force from which no one is exempt" (*Design* 165). Semiotics, cultural criticism, and visual literacy have contributed much to our understanding of the sophistication of the visual environment around us and the ways by which we interact with images and artifacts to build and reaffirm our cultural assumptions.

Semiotics. *Semiotics* is the study of signs—not traffic signs but things that stand for someone or something else. Based on the linguistic theories of Ferdinand de Saussure and others, semiotics, or semiology, has been very influential in interpreting the visual in our culture. The theorist Roland Barthes has contributed, among many other studies, an interpretation of the Eiffel Tower as an iconic part of visual life. Arthur Asa Berger's *Media Analysis Techniques* (1991) surveys semiotic approaches to advertising and television. Gunther Kress and Theo van Leeuwen have offered a sweeping social semiotic description of images from newspaper layouts to film to charts and graphs in *Reading Images: The Grammar of Visual Design* (1996).

Cultural and ideological criticism. In its broadest sense, cultural criticism offers a vocabulary and set of concepts from many fields—such as history, art history, philosophy, and anthropology—to analyze the visual world in intellectual terms. The work of art historian Ernst Gombrich on representation, using examples from *New Yorker* cartoons to medieval drawings, continues to be influential in the study of visuals with its social approach. In the area of technology, Jay David Bolter's *Writing Space: The Computer, Hypertext, and the History of Writing* (1991), especially the chapter "Seeing and Writing," touches many of the problems that face the writer who is becoming aware of visual communication. Although *Writing Space* predates the World Wide Web, it is particularly good at placing Western ideas of print and illustration in a large historical sweep from classical times to the present. Bolter also notes the influence of phonetic literacy and print technology on our present understanding of visuals.

The power relationships that we construct and maintain through our texts, visuals, and cultural artifacts are the subject of ideological criticism. John Berger's *Ways of Seeing* allies the traditional history of painting with media criticism. There is a large body of feminist critique of advertising and the visual arts as well, such as Rosemary Betterton's 1987 collection. The ideological critique of graphic design is often treated with industrial design because consumer products have become almost indistinguishable from their packaging and marketing. Adrian

Forty's *Objects of Desire* (1986) discusses, among other artifacts, the subtle advertising of the now-famous London subway map. Ellen Lupton, a museum curator and exhibition designer, has explored the industrial design of consumer products and the architecture of bathrooms and waste systems, as well as popular graphic design. For example, with J. Abbott Miller, Lupton has analyzed images of race, gender, age, and beauty in stock photography, now widely available in digital form and even packaged with software. A collection of short analyses edited by Steven Heller and Karen Pomeroy takes on graphic design from Hitler to *Mad* magazine. Cynthia Y. Selfe and Richard J. Selfe, Jr., explore the politics of computer interfaces. Geographer Mark Monmonier's works on maps critique the power relationships of information graphics. In *Remediation: Understanding New Media,* Jay David Bolter and Richard Grusin present a wide-ranging theoretical study of visual representation that includes computer games, photography, digital art, film, virtual reality, theme parks, television, and the Web.

Visual literacy. The number and kinds of images that children see and their responses to these images make up another important issue. The phrase "visual literacy," once used mainly in education, now is loosely applied to the study of all types of visuals, from information graphics to video and film. One figure associated with visual literacy is professor of mass communications Paul Messaris. The International Visual Literacy Association maintains a large bibliography (with materials up to 1995) at its Web site.

Rhetoric, document design, usability studies, and professional communication

Writers have typically been *logocentric*—centered on words, not visuals (Schriver 72). Yet for some time, writing scholars have brought semiotic and ideological theory to the visual nature of texts. Through a growing awareness of "document design," they have also brought another strand of thought to bear on visual communication: empirical research in the ways that readers perceive and respond to the look of documents. Technical and professional writing has particularly contributed in this area. Above all, the field of writing views visuals as rhetorical, embedded in the relationships of writer (or designer), reader, and purpose.

The document design and usability testing movements. In the 1960's and 1970's, citizens' rights advocates began calling for the clear communication of information about consumer products and government services (Schriver 26). In the United States, this "plain language" movement resulted in federal and state initiatives to reduce paperwork and communicate in clear, simple language. Although these initiatives had lost momentum by the 1980's, they gave rise to research projects that linked industry consultants, research psychologists, and scholars of English and writing. This collaboration has affected the structure of these fields to this day.

In particular, the document design movement brought layout and visuals to writers' attention as integral to communication. The monograph *Guidelines for Document Designers* (1981), the textbook *Writing in the Professions* (1981), and the scholarly collection *Writing in Non-Academic Settings* (1985), all co-authored or edited by members of the original Document Design Project, have introduced many writing teachers to a structured, research-based rationale for design advice.

One outgrowth of document design research has come to be known as ***usability testing***. Employing a wide range of research techniques from cognitive and human factors psychology as well as ethnographic and sociological methods, usability testing enables writers to discover users' goals and needs in documents (Duin 307). In its focus on readers, usability testing is rhetorical, and often involves visual communication. Manuals, computer documentation, and interfaces are the main materials tested, but the philosophy that writers should be advocates for readers has affected many other types of public documents. *The Design of Everyday Things*, by Donald A. Norman, an industrial psychologist, is an interesting and accessible treatment of human factors and user-centered design issues.

The fields of usability testing and human factors have become increasingly important for visual communicators, especially Web site designers. For conducting serious usability research, there is *A Practical Guide to Usability Testing* by Joseph S. Dumas and Janice C. Redish. Writers interested in the brain's processing of visual and other information can profit from examining Marlana Coe's *Human Factors for Technical Communicators*. The growing literature on *information visualization*, discussed earlier, is also relevant. For accessible Web sites, Jakob Nielsen's online column entitled "Alertbox" (www.useit.com) has become a standard, although many Web designers find his advice too restrictive. Nielsen, formerly an engineer for Sun Microsystems, has also published a book, *Designing Web Usability: The Practice of Simplicity*. Steve Krug has written a straightforward treatment of online accessibility in *Don't Make Me Think!: A Common Sense Approach to Web Usability*.

Professional and technical communication. Textbooks in technical and business communication have long included information graphics and now usually include a section on document design. Increasingly, visual communication is regarded as a field of study and a number of programs have courses in visual rhetoric or visual communication (Alred 137-43). Scholars who have examined the visual include Stephen Bernhardt, Ben F. Barton, and Marthalee

171

S. Barton. Recently two research-based texts by Karen A. Schriver (1997) and Charles Kostelnick and David D. Roberts (1998) have been all or substantially devoted to visual communication.

Summary

- Visual communication has social, technological, and intellectual contexts in graphic design and other fields.
- Modernism and postmodernism have influenced the look of contemporary documents.
- Other influences on the practice and theory of visuals come from information graphics, visual problem solving, semiotics, cultural and ideological criticism, the visual literacy movement, rhetoric, document design research, and professional communication.

Exercises

Invite a panel to discuss the visual design of publications. You might start by considering people in these areas:

- publications editor for campus newspaper or magazine
- scholarly editor from the humanities, arts, sciences, or engineering
- director of campus publicity
- Webmaster for an organization
- freelance graphic artist
- local printer

Ask them to bring one or two representative publications (the Webmaster will need online access) that they are prepared to discuss. Here are a few questions that you might ask them to prepare for:

- What education and experience led them to this type of position?
- What kinds of visuals are they most familiar with?
- How do they usually interpret those visuals?
- What guidelines do they use for the format and look of publications?
- Who makes decisions about the look?

- What is the process of publication?
- What advice do they commonly give writers about creating visuals and producing attractive, informative documents?

Notes

[1]There are many other aspects of modernism in art and literature. For an explanation of modern art's impact on graphic design, see Meggs, "The Influence of Modern Art," *A History of Graphic Design*, pp. 238-55.

Glossary

Numbers in parentheses ( ) indicate the chapter or chapters where the term is discussed.

aesthetics. The study of art and beauty. (9)

arrangement. In a document, the process of ordering information persuasively. Arrangement is the second stage of classical rhetoric. (1)

bar chart. A chart with horizontal bars, allowing comparison of values across categories. (3)

body type. Fonts that can be read at length and used in text passages. (6)

chart. A graphical display of numerical information. (3, 7)

chartjunk. Extraneous detail in charts. (7)

chunking. Breaking information into small, visually distinct sections. (1, 2)

clip art. Widely available generic drawings used to add interest to documents. (3)

cognitive styles. Learning styles. (2)

color cueing. Using colors to focus attention, simplify information, group elements, and create separate layers of information. (1)

column chart. A chart with vertical bars. (3)

column heading. In a table, the top row that gives important information. (3)

conceptual photograph. A photograph that is posed or manipulated to make a point. (3)

contour lines. Lines that show changes in elevation in a topographic map. (3)

contrast. How well items stand out from each other and the background. See also **figure-ground separation**. (2)

convention. A customary feature that readers expect to appear in a particular genre. (2)

creating multiple paths. Giving readers both verbal and visual choices throughout a document to support their different experiences and learning styles. (1)

cropping. Cutting extraneous details from the edges of an image. (3)

cultural criticism. The analysis of visual and other cultural artifacts using the methods of history, art history, philosophy, psychology, anthropology, and other fields.

data displays, data graphics. See **information graphics**. (3)

data map. Shows statistical information across an area, such as the density of population. (3)

data set. The total body of numerical data from which a particular information graphic is drawn. (3)

delivery. The last stage in classical rhetoric, which includes the placement of text and visuals, plus choices of type, color, and details of paper, ink, and binding (for print documents) or platform and interface (for screen documents). Also called **production.** (1, 9)

dingbat. A small visual symbol. (5)

direction. The slant of strokes in a typeface. (6)

discourse communities. Groups of readers and writers with a common knowledge of language and conventions. (2)

display type. Fonts suited for titles and headings. Display type includes decorative, unusual, and script fonts, as well as all bold, heavy fonts. (6)

distribution map. Shows the location (or distribution) of features across an area, such as average temperatures. (3)

document design. Use of verbal and visual features that have been shown to be easily understood by readers. (1, 9)

documents. Paper and on-screen writing, also referred to as text. (1)

drop cap. An enlarged capital letter that leads readers into an article. (6)

drop shadow. A type feature that looks like a cast shadow, used to create interest and increase figure-ground contrast. (5)

ethos. The credibility or character of the writer as it is projected through the document. One of the three **rhetorical appeals** of classical rhetoric. (1, 4, 9)

event map. Follows a sequence of events from place to place, with commentary. (3)

expressive purpose. Engaging the reader through personal values, opinions, and interests. (4)

fair use. A federal policy that allows writers limited use of the copyrighted works of others, without asking permission of the copyright owner. (7)

figure-ground separation. The ability to see an image against a background, one of the most fundamental aspects of visual perception. A Gestalt principle. (2)

filtering. Focusing on design features like headings, lists, typographic changes, and layout while ignoring other sensory information. (1, 2)

focal point. In perception, an area that we focus our eyes on. Within any visual field, we tend to find only a few focal points. (2)

font. The design of a particular set of type. Also called **typeface.** (6)

foveal vision. The small, jumping movement of the eyes to bring visual input onto the fovea, the area of clearest vision. (2)

genre. Kind of discourse or document, a "socially active" device to help readers determine what the writer wants from them. (2)

genre knowledge. The networks of mental models or schemata that we have created from repeated experiences. (2)

geologic map. Shows the strata below the earth's surface. (3)

Gestalt. A German word that is translated as "form" or "wholeness." (2)

graphic design. Using typography, illustration, photography, and printing to persuade, interest, and inform. (9)

graphics. Visuals that are distinct from verbal material. Also referred to as **images**. (1)

grid. Division of a page or screen into rectangular areas as a template for page or screen layout. (5)

grouping. Creating visual relationships between items. (2)

hue. What is usually meant by color, such as blue, green, or red. (2)

icon. A small, stylized image. Icons are often used in making electronic links or "buttons." (3, 9)

ideological criticism. The study of power relationships that we construct and maintain through our texts, visuals, and cultural artifacts. Includes feminist and Marxist criticism. (9)

image. A visual that is distinct from text, also referred to as a graphic. In particular, photographs, drawings, cartoons, and ads. (1, 3)

image memory. Memory of particular visual images plus our constructed "mental images" of pictures, events, and visual-related words. One of the most enduring types of memory. (2)

information graphics. Visuals such as tables, charts, graphs, and maps. Sometimes called **data graphics** or **data displays**. (3)

invention. The first stage of classical rhetoric, which includes planning, audience analysis, and developing the overall approach to a document. (1, 4)

inverted-L. A common format for Web pages that places the title/logo (and often other elements, such as a navigation bar) across the top of the screen and a table of contents area along the left edge of the screen. (5, 8)

jumpline. Text at the bottom center or bottom right of an article that indicates continuation onto another page. (5)

justification. Alignment of both the left and right edges of text passages by inserting small amounts of extra space between words. Also called **full justification**. (6)

key or **legend.** Interprets the graphic symbols of a map. (3)

land use map. Shows human activity in an area, such as industry, residences, farmland, and parks. (3)

layering. Creating visual objects through a document that can be scanned separately from surrounding text. (1, 2)

leading. Pronounced "ledding." The vertical spacing between lines of type. (6)

letterform. In a font, the visual structure of an individual letter. (6)

letterbox. An increasingly popular Web page format that emphasizes graphics. The middle area of the screen is a wide horizontal "letterbox," with a title/logo area above and a navigation area below. (5)

letterspacing. Putting small amounts of extra space between letters for a decorative effect. (6)

line graph. A chart using lines to show trends, usually over time. (3)

location map. Shows an area featured in a news story. (3)

logo. A visual symbol identifying a group. (4)

logos. The reasoning of a document. One of the three **rhetorical appeals** of classical rhetoric. (1, 4)

logotype. A logo combined with text, as in a letterhead. (4)

map. A graphical representation of the landscape and its features. (3)

Mercator projection. A standard form of world map that enlarges areas near the poles. (3)

mixing modes. Giving information in pictures as well as words. (1)

modernism. Influential group of artistic and intellectual movements that emphasize function, simplicity of form, universality, objectivity, and intuition. (9)

multimedia design. Using text, graphics, video, and sound in a presentation or document. (9)

multi-panel genres. Documents that unfold through time as readers turn pages, open folded sections, or click on links. (4, 5)

news and documentary photos. Spontaneous or near-spontaneous recordings of human events and conditions, ranging from news events to sports to daily life. (3)

Old Style. A traditional style of font with graceful curved lines and serifs. (6)

orientation. An object's direction—upright, horizontal, slanted, or rotated. (2)

pathos. The reader's emotional response to and intensity of interest in a document. One of the three **rhetorical appeals** of classical rhetoric. (1, 4)

pictograph. A picture representing a word or idea. (9)

pie chart. A chart that shows how a whole is divided into parts. (3)

pixellation. Jagged, dot-like appearance of letters. (6)

poetic or artistic purpose. Engaging the reader in a playful or aesthetic experience. (4)

point. A measure of the height of a typeface, approximately 1/72 of an inch. (6)

postmodernism. Intellectual and artistic movements that challenge the assumptions of modernism. (9)

production. The techniques and process of putting a document into final form for readers. Also see **delivery.** (4)

projection. Technique used by mapmakers to convert the three-dimensional surface of the earth into the two dimensions of a flat plane. (3)

proximity. The Gestalt principle of placing related objects close to each other. (2, 5)

pull quote. A quotation "pulled" from an article, separated and highlighted to attract attention on a page. (5, 8)

queuing. Creating visual hierarchies of information, as through headings and subheadings. (1, 2)

reading goal. One of five ways that readers approach documents: skimming, scanning, searching, reading receptively, or reading critically. (2)

reversed type. Putting white or light letters on a dark background. (6)

rhetorical appeal. In classical rhetoric, a persuasive strategy: logos, ethos, or pathos. (1, 4)

rhetoric. The interaction of writers and readers in effective communication. (1, 9)

rule. A horizontal line. (5)

sans serif font. A contemporary-looking typeface without serifs or stress. (6, 9)

saturation. The purity of a hue. Bright red is highly saturated, while pink is not. (2)

scale. The proportion of distances on the map to distances on the ground. (3)

schema. A mental model. (1)

script. Type that imitates the look of handwriting. (6)

semiotics. The study of signs, based on the linguistic theories of Ferdinand de Saussure and others. (9)

serifs. Strokes on the ends of letters. (6)

similarity. The Gestalt principle of grouping objects by shape, orientation, color, or texture. (2, 5)

single-panel genres. Documents that readers generally see "all at once." (4, 5)

squint test. Squinting at a page or screen to blur the details and make the overall design elements stand out. (5)

stacked column charts and **stacked area charts**. Charts that show both trends and the contribution of individual components to a total. (3)

stock photographs. Widely available conceptual photographs used to add interest and polish to documents. (3)

storyboard. A sequence of thumbnails (quick sketches) with commentary, useful for planning multi-panel genres like newsletters and Web pages. (4)

stress. In a font, having both thick and thin strokes within a letter. (6)

stub. In a table, the far-left column that labels the rows. (3)

style. The third stage of classical rhetoric, which concerns choosing appropriate details in wording or design features. (1)

surface map. Shows the location of places on the earth's surface: highways, streets, airports, towns, points of interest. (3)

table. An arrangement of words or numbers into columns and rows. (3, 7)

template. Preset model of a genre (such as a resume or Web page) provided by a word processing or desktop publishing program to help writers lay out a document. (5)

text. Paper and on-screen writing, also referred to as a document. (1)

texture. A pattern on an object. (2)

thumbnail. A small, quick, rough sketch used for planning visuals. (4)

tonal desity. The total amount of ink on the page or a section of a page; a term from printing.

topographic map. Shows visible features of the earth, such as mountains and rivers, often with contour lines. (3)

transactional purpose. Expecting readers to treat the information and claims of a document as truthful so they can take further action. (4)

type. In printing, all alphabetic and numerical characters, plus punctuation marks. (6)

typeface. See **font.**

usability testing or field testing. In technical writing and interface design, a structured form of getting reader input. (4, 9)

user-centered design. Engaging readers in the process of designing documents through design reviews and user testing. (1, 9)

value. The amount of black or white in a color—its lightness or darkness. An important concept for designing documents. (2, 5)

visual communication. The ways in which the writers and readers interact through the look of the pages and screens. (1)

visual convention. A visual feature that readers expect to appear in a particular genre. (2)

visual design. The structured process of planning for visual communication. (1)

visual field. In perception, the entire expanse of space visible at one time without moving the eyes. (2)

visual literacy. The ability to analyze and interpret visuals in our culture. (3, 9)

visual perception. The active process of planning for as well as interpreting sensory data from the eyes. (2)

weather map. Shows the distribution of temperatures and the weather forecast. (3)

weight. In a font, the thickness of strokes. (6)

x-axis. The horizontal dimension on most common charts. (3)

x-height. In a typeface, the height of small letters like *e* and *x*. X-height is a major factor in legibility. (6)

y-axis. The vertical dimension on most common charts. (3)

Works Cited

Alred, Gerald J. *The St. Martin's Bibliography of Business and Technical Communication.* New York: St. Martin's, 1997.

Appignasnesi, Richard, and Chris Garratt. *Introducing Postmodernism.* New York: Totem, 1995.

Arnheim, Rudolf. *Visual Thinking.* Berkeley, CA: U of Cal. P, 1969.

Aziz, Barbara Nimri. "Maps and the Mind." *Human Nature* 1 (Aug. 1978): 50-59.

Baird, Russell N., Duncan McDonald, Ronald H. Pittman, and Arthur T. Turnbull. *The Graphics of Communication: Methods, Media and Technology.* 6th ed. Fort Worth: Harcourt, 1993.

Bang, Molly. *Picture This: Perception and Composition.* Foreword by Rudolf Arnheim. Boston: Bulfinch-Little, Brown, 1991.

Barthes, Roland. *Image, Music, Text.* Trans. Stephen Heath. New York: Hill and Wang, 1977.

Barton, Ben F., and Marthalee S. Barton. "Ideology and the Map: Toward a Postmodern Design Practice." *Professional Communication: The Social Perspective.* Ed. Nancy Roundy Blyler and Charlotte Thralls. Newbury Park, CA: Sage, 1993. 49-78.

———. "Postmodernism and the Relation of Word and Image in Professional Discourse." *Technical Writing Teacher* 17.3 (1990): 256-70.

Berger, Arthur Asa. "Sex and Symbol in Fashion Advertising and Analyzing Signs and Systems," in Diana George and John Trimbur, *Reading Culture: Contexts for Critical Reading and Writing,* 3rd ed. New York: Longman, 1999. Pp. 186-93;.

Berger, John. *Ways of Seeing.* London: BBC-Penguin, 1972.

Bernhardt, Stephen A. "Seeing the Text." *College Composition and Communication* 37.1 (1986): 68-78.

———. "The Design of Sexism: The Case of an Army Maintenance Manual." *IEEE Transactions on Professional Communication* 35.4 (1992): 217-21.

Bertin, Jacques. *Semiology of Graphics: Diagrams Networks Maps.* Trans. William J. Berg. Madison: U of Wisconsin P, 1983.

Betterton, Rosemary, ed. *Looking On: Images of Femininity in the Visual Arts and Media.* London: Pandora, 1987.

Bolter, Jay David. *Writing Space: The Computer, Hypertext, and the History of Writing.* Hillsdale, NJ: Erlbaum, 1991.

Bolter, Jay David, and Richard Grusin. *Remediation: Understanding New Media.* Cambridge, MA: MIT Press, 1999.

Brasseur, Lee. Review of *Visual Explanations: Images and Quantities, Evidence and Narrative. Technical Communication Quarterly.* 7.3 (1998): 341-45.

Britton, James, et al. *The Development of Writing Abilities (11-18).* Schools Council Research Studies. London: Macmillan, 1975.

Card, Stuart A., Jock D. Mackinlay, and Ben Shneiderman. *Readings in Information Visualization: Using Vision to Think.* San Francisco, CA: Morgan Kaufman, 1999.

Coe, Marlana. *Human Factors for Technical Communicators.* Wiley Technical Communication Library. New York: John Wiley & Sons, 1996.

Day, Robert A. *How to Write and Publish a Scientific Paper.* 4nd ed. Phoenix: Oryx, 1994.

De Bono, Edward. *New Think: The Use of Lateral Thinking in the Generation of New Ideas.* New York: Basic Books, 1968.

Dragga, Sam, and Gwendolyn Gong. *Editing: The Design of Rhetoric.* Amityville, NY: Baywood, 1989.

Duin, Ann Hill. "Test Drive—Evaluating the Usability of Documents." *Techniques for Technical Communicators.* Ed. Carol M. Barnum and Saul Carliner. New York: Macmillan, 1993. 306-35.

Dumas, Joseph S., and Janice C. Redish. *A Practical Guide to Usability Testing.* Exeter, England: Intellect, 1999.

Edwards, Betty. *Drawing on the Right Side of the Brain: A Course in Enhancing Creativity and Artistic Confidence.* Los Angeles: Tarcher-St. Martin's, 1979.

Felker, Daniel B., Frances Pickering, Veda R. Charrow, V. Melissa Holland, and Janice C. Redish. *Guidelines for Document Designers.* Washington, DC: Amer. Inst. for Research, n.d.

Finberg, Howard I., and Bruce D. Itule. *Visual Editing: A Graphic Guide for Journalists.* Belmont, CA: Wadsworth, 1990.

Forty, Adrian. *Objects of Desire: Design and Society from Wedgwood to IBM.* London: Pantheon, 1986.

Gardner, Howard. *Frames of Mind: The Theory of Multiple Intelligences.* New York: Basic, 1983.

Giannetti, Louis D., and John W. Langdon. *Understanding Movies.* 8th ed. New York: Prentice Hall, 1998.

Gibaldi, Joseph. *MLA Handbook for Writers of Research Papers.* 4th ed. New York: Mod. Lang. Assn., 1995.

Gombrich, E. H. *Art and Illusion: A Study in the Psychology of Pictorial Representation*. Princeton, NJ: Princeton UP, 1969.

Hawisher, Gail E., and Cynthia L.Selfe. *Literacy, Technology, and Society: Confronting the Issues*. Upper Saddle River, NJ: Prentice Hall, 1997.

Heller, Steven, and Karen Pomeroy. *Design Literacy: Understanding Graphic Design*. New York: Allworth, 1997.

Horton, William. *Illustrating Computer Documentation*. New York: Wiley, 1991.

Huff, Darrell. *How to Lie with Statistics*. New York: Norton, 1954.

International Visual Literacy Association. "IVLA: Research Documents." http://www.ivla.org/news/rdocs/index.htm. (5 Feb. 1999).

Jolliffe, David A. "Genre." *Encyclopedia of Rhetoric and Composition: Communication from Ancient Times to the Information Age*. Ed. Theresa Enos. New York: Garland, 1996. 279-84.

Keyes, Elizabeth. "Typography, Color, and Information Structure." *Technical Communication* 40 (1993): 640-49

Killingsworth, M. Jimmie, and Jacqueline S. Palmer. *Information in Action: A Guide to Technical Communication*. 2nd ed. Boston: Allyn and Bacon, 1999.

Kinross, Robin. "The Rhetoric of Neutrality." *Design Discourse: History, Theory, Criticism*. Victor Margolin, ed. Chicago: U of Chicago P, 1989. 131-43.

Kosslyn, Stephen M. *Elements of Graph Design*. New York: Freeman, 1994.

Kostelnick, Charles. "Conflicting Standards for Designing Data Displays: Following, Flouting, and Reconciling Them. *Technical Communication* 45.4 (1998): 473-82.

———. "Cultural Adaptation and Information Design: Two Contrasting Views." *IEEE Transactions on Professional Communication* 38.4 (1995): 182-96.

———. "The Rhetoric of Text Design in Professional Communication." *Technical Writing Teacher* 17.3 (1990): 189-202.

———. "Typographical Design, Modernist Aesthetics, and Professional Communication." *Journal of Business and Technical Communication* 4.1 (1990): 5-24.

Kostelnick, Charles, and David D. Roberts. *Designing Visual Language: Strategies for Professional Communicators*. Boston: Allyn & Bacon, 1998.

Kress, Gunther, and Theo van Leeuwen. *Reading Images: The Grammar of Visual Design*. London: Routledge, 1996.

Kristof, Ray, and Amy Satran. *Interactivity by Design: Creating and Communicating with New Media*. Mountain View, CA: Adobe, 1995.

Krug, Steve. *Don't Make Me Think!: A Common Sense Approach to Web Usability*. Indianapolis: Que, 2000.

Lopuck, Lisa. *Designing Multimedia: A Visual Guide to Multimedia and Online Graphic Design*. Berkeley, CA: Peachpit, 1996.

Lupton, Ellen, and J. Abbott Miller. *Design Writing Research: Writing on Graphic Design*. New York: Princeton Architectural, 1996.

———. *The Bathroom, the Kitchen and the Aesthetics of Waste: A Process of Elimination*. New York: Princeton Architectural, 1992.

Maitra, Kaushiki, and Dixie Goswami. "Responses of American Readers to Visual Aspects of a Mid-Sized Japanese Company's Annual Report: A Case Study." *IEEE Transactions on Professional Communication* 38.4 (1995): 197-203.

Margolin, Victor, ed. *Design Discourse: History, Theory, Criticism*. Chicago: U of Chicago P, 1989.

McKim, Robert H. *Thinking Visually: A Strategy Manual for Problem Solving*. Belmont, CA: Wadsworth, 1980.

McNaughton, Sean. "Information Graphics at the *Boston Globe*: From Concept to Execution." *Technical Communication* 45.4 (1998): 483-90.

Meggs, Philip. *A History of Graphic Design*. 2nd ed. New York: Van Nostrand Reinhold, 1992.

Messaris, Paul. *Visual Persuasion: The Role of Images in Advertising*. Thousand Oaks, CA: Sage, 1997.

Miller, Carolyn R. "Genre as Social Action." *Quarterly Journal of Speech* 70.2 (1984): 151-67.

Monmonier, Mark. *How to Lie with Maps*. Chicago: U of Chicago P, 1991.

Mullet, Kevin, and Darrell Sano. *Designing Visual Interfaces: Communication Oriented Techniques*. Mountain View, CA: Sunsoft-Prentice Hall, 1995.

Nielsen, Jakob. "The Alertbox: Current Issues in User Interface Design." http://www.useit.com/alertbox/ (5 Oct 1998).

Nielsen, Jakob, *Designing Web Usability: The Practice of Simplicity*. Indianapolis: New Riders, 2000.

Nicolaides, Kimon. *The Natural Way to Draw: A Working Plan for Art Study*. New York: Houghton, 1990.

Norman, Donald A. *The Design of Everyday Things*. New York: Currency-Doubleday, 1990.

Odell, Lee, Dixie Goswami, Anne Herrington, and Doris Quick. "Studying Writing in Non-Academic Settings." *New Essays in Technical and Scientific Communication: Research, Theory, Practice.* Ed. Paul V. Anderson, R. John Brockmann, and Carolyn R. Miller. Farmingtondale, NY: Baywood, 1983. 17-40.

Parker, Roger C. *The Makeover Book: 101 Design Solutions for Desktop Publishing.* Chapel Hill: Ventana, 1989.

Penrose, Ann M., and Steven B. Katz. *Writing in the Sciences: Exploring Conventions of Scientific Discourse.* New York: St. Martin's, 1998.

Publication Manual of the American Psychological Association. 4th ed. Washington, DC: Amer. Psychological Assn., 1994.

"A Raven as Designed by Committee." *New York Times Magazine* 10 Nov. 1996: 50.

Redish, Janice C. "Understanding Readers." *Techniques for Technical Communicators.* Ed. Carol M. Barnum and Saul Carliner. New York: Macmillan, 1993. 14-41.

Shneiderman, Ben. *Designing the User Interface: Strategies for Effective Human-Computer Interaction.* 3rd ed. Reading, MA: Addison-Wesley, 1998.

Schriver, Karen A. *Dynamics in Document Design: Creating Texts for Readers.* New York: Wiley, 1997.

Selfe, Cynthia L., and Richard J. Selfe, Jr. "The Politics of the Interface: Power and Its Exercises in Electronic Contact Zones." *College Composition and Communication* 45.4 (1994): 484-504.

Tinker, Miles A. *Legibility of Print.* Ames, IA: Iowa State University P, 1963.

Tufte, Edward R. *The Visual Display of Quantitative Information.* Cheshire, CT: Graphics, 1983.

———. *Visual Explanations: Images and Quantities, Evidence and Narrative.* Cheshire, CT: Graphics, 1997.

Ware, Colin. *Information Visualization: Perception for Design.* San Francisco: Morgan Kaufman, 2000.

Williams, Robin. *The Non-Designer's Design Book: Design and Typographic Principles for the Visual Novice.* Berkeley, CA: Peachpit, 1994.

Williams, Robin, and John Tollett. *A Blip in the Continuum.* Berkeley, CA: Peachpit, 1995.